Walt Whitman's Songs of Male Intimacy and Love

The
Iowa
Whitman
Series

ED FOLSOM

series editor

Walt Whitman's Songs of Male Intimacy and Love

"Live Oak, with Moss" and "Calamus"

Edited by Betsy Erkkila

UNIVERSITY OF IOWA PRESS, IOWA CITY

University of Iowa Press, Iowa City 52242
Copyright © 2011 by the University of Iowa Press
www.uiowapress.org
Printed in the United States of America
Design by Richard Hendel

The University of Iowa Press is a member of
Green Press Initiative and is committed to preserving
natural resources.

Printed on acid-free paper

Library of Congress
Cataloging-in-Publication Data
Whitman, Walt, 1819–1892.
[Poems. Selections.]
Walt Whitman's songs of male intimacy and love: "Live oak,
with moss" and "Calamus" / edited by Betsy Erkkila.
p.   cm.—(The Iowa Whitman series, ISSN 1556-5610)
Includes bibliographical references.
Summary: This volume includes Whitman's handwritten
manuscript version of the twelve "Live oak, with moss" poems
alongside a print transcription of these poems on the opposite page,
followed by a facsimile of the original version of the "Calamus"
poems published in the 1860–61 edition of Leaves of grass,
and a reprint of the final version of the "Calamus" poems
in the 1881 edition of Leaves of grass.
ISBN-13: 978-1-58729-958-2 (pbk.), ISBN-10: 1-58729-958-5 (pbk.)
ISBN-13: 978-1-58729-959-9 (ebk.), ISBN-10: 1-58729-959-3 (ebk.)
1. Homosexuality—Poetry.   I. Erkkila, Betsy, 1944–
II. Whitman, Walt, 1819–1892. Live oak, with moss.
III. Whitman, Walt, 1819–1892. Calamus.   IV. Title.
PS3204.E75 2011
811'.3—dc22   2010038901

To Robert K. Martin

I will lift what has too long kept down those
*   smouldering fires,*
I will give them complete abandonment,
I will write the evangel-poem of comrades, and of love,
(For who but I should understand love, with all its
*   sorrow and joy?*
And who but I should be the poet of comrades?)

Walt Whitman, "Proto-Leaf"

CONTENTS

Manly Love in All Its Moods: A Preface
xi

Live Oak, with Moss
1

Calamus, 1860
39

Calamus, 1881
79

Songs of Male Intimacy and Love:
An Afterword
99

"Calamus" and Whitman's Man Love:
A Selected Bibliography
163

MANLY LOVE IN ALL ITS MOODS
A Preface

In "Live Oak, with Moss," Whitman's unpublished sheaf of twelve poems on manly passion and love written in 1859, the poet dreams of a city—a public urban space—where men who love men can live and love openly in accord with their desires. One hundred and fifty years after Whitman expressed this dream as part of a fully realized democracy in the United States and elsewhere, Whitman's own country is still locked in a struggle over whether men who love men have the same civil and legal rights as men who love women. These public contests over the visibility, equality, and rights of men who love men have been at the very center of contests over the life, work, and legacy of Walt Whitman, America's (and the world's) major poet of democracy and its major singer of what he called "manly love" in all its moods—from unutterable loss, pain, sorrow, depression, and social death to orgasmic and spiritual communion, joy, bliss, song, and celebration.

Whitman's "Calamus"—his cluster of poems on "adhesive" and manly love, comradeship, and democracy—was first published in the 1860–61 edition of *Leaves of Grass*. Although the book was published in 1860, Whitman dated it "1860–61" so that his book could commemorate the eighty-fifth anniversary of the Declaration of Independence (he thus invented a new American calendar, as he recorded on his title page that his date of publication was "Year 85 of These States"). It is to honor and commemorate the first publication of the "Calamus" poems in the 1860–61 edition that I publish the little-known manuscript of notebook poems, "Live Oak, with Moss," the 1860–61 "Calamus" poems, and the final 1881 "Calamus" poems together in a single edition for the first time. In addition to honoring the sesquicentennial of the "Calamus" cluster, this volume seeks to mark and celebrate the sexual and political radicalism and ongoing power, influence, and legacy of Whitman's songs of manly passion, sex, and love.

The volume begins with Whitman's clean and elegantly handwritten manuscript version of the twelve "Live Oak, with Moss" poems, which are printed side by side with a print transcription of these poems on the opposite page. The "Live Oak" poems are followed by a facsimile of the original version of the "Calamus" poems published in the 1860–61 edition of *Leaves of Grass*. The concluding section of poems reprints the final version of the "Calamus" poems in the 1881 edition of *Leaves of Grass*. In an afterword, I discuss the radical nature of these poems in literary, sexual, and social history, the changes Whitman made in the "Live Oak" and "Calamus" poems in the post-Civil War and Reconstruction years, the literary, political, and other contests surrounding these poems, and the constitutive role these poems have played in the emergence of modern sexual and homosexual identity and the ongoing struggle for sexual freedom, tolerance, rights, and democracy for man-loving men in the United States and worldwide. The volume closes with a selected bibliography of works that have contributed to the critical and interpretive contests around Whitman's man-loving life, works, and legacy.

The "Live Oak, with Moss" facsimile is reproduced here with the permission of the Alderman Library at the University of Virginia.

Live Oak, with Moss

Live Oak, with Moss.

II.

Not the heat flames up and con-
    sumes,
Not the sea=waves hurry in and
    out,
Not the air, delicious and dry, the
    air of the ripe summer, bears
    lightly along white down=balls
    of myriads of seeds, wafted
    sailing gracefully, to drop
    where they may,
Not these — O none of these, more
    than the flames of me, con-
    suming, burning for his love
    whom I love — O none more
    than I hurrying in and out;
Does the tide hurry, seeking some-
    thing, and never give up? — O
    I, the same, to seek my life=long
    lover;
O nor down=balls nor perfumes, nor
    the high rain=emitting clouds,
    are borne through the open air,
    more than my copious soul is
    borne through the open air, wafted
    in all directions, for friendship, for
    love. —

(2)

Calamus-Leaves

Live Oak, with Moss

I.

Not the heat flames up and con-
      sumes,
Not the sea-waves hurry in and
      out,
Not the air, delicious and dry, the
      air of the ripe summer, bears
      lightly along white down-balls
      of myriads of seeds, wafted,
      sailing gracefully, to drop
      where they may,
Not these—O none of these, more
      than the flames of me, con-
      suming, burning for his love
      whom I love—O none, more
      than I, hurrying in and out;
Does the tide hurry, seeking some-
      thing, and never give up?—O
      I, the same, to seek my life-long
      lover;
O nor down-balls, nor perfumes, nor
      the high rain-emitting clouds,
      are borne through the open air,
      more than my copious soul is
      borne through the open air, wafted
      in all directions, for friendship, for
      love.—

II

I saw in Louisiana a
live-oak growing,
All alone stood it, and the
moss hung down from the
branches,
Without any companion it grew
there, glistening out with
joyous leaves of dark green,
And its look, rude, unbending,
lusty, made me think of
myself;
But I wondered how it could
utter joyous leaves, standing
alone there without its friend,
its lover — For I knew I could
not;
And I plucked a twig with
a certain number of leaves
upon it, and twined around
it a little moss, and brought
it away — And I have placed
it in sight in my room,

2

(4)

II

I saw in Louisiana a
     live-oak growing,
All alone stood it, and the
     moss hung down from the
     branches,
Without any companion it grew
     there, glistening out
     joyous leaves of dark green,
And its look, rude, unbending,
     lusty, made me think of
     myself;
But I wondered how it could
     utter joyous leaves, standing
     alone there without its friend,
     its lover – For I knew I could
     not;
And I plucked a twig with
     a certain number of leaves
     upon it, and twined around
     it a little moss, and brought
     it away — And I have placed
     it in sight in my room,

It is not needed to remind
me as of my friends, (for I
believe lately think of little
else than of them,)
Yet it remains to me a
curious token – it makes
me think of manly love,
these pieces, and name
them after it;
For all that, and though the
live oak glistens there in Louis-
iana, solitary in a wide
flat space, uttering joyous
leaves all its life, without
a friend, a lover, near – I
know very well I could
not.

It is not needed to remind
        me as of my friends, (for I
        believe lately I think of little
        else than of them,)
Yet it remains to me a
        curious token—it makes
        me think of manly love;
For all that, and though the
        live oak glistens there in Louis-
        iana, solitary in a wide
        flat space, uttering joyous
        leaves all its life, without
        a friend, a lover, near—I
        know very well I could
        not.

⫴

When I heard at the close of
      the day how I had been
      praised in the Capitol, still
      it was not a happy night
      for me that followed;
And ~~else~~ Nor, when I caroused — Or
— Nor when my favorite ~~plans~~ were accom-
      plished — ~~it was well enough~~ was I really happy
      ~~Still I was not happy;~~
But ~~that~~ the day the that when I rose
      at dawn from the bed of
      perfect health, electric, in-
      haling sweet breath,
When I saw the full moon
      in the west grow pale and
      disappear in the morning light,
When I wandered alone over the
      beach and undressing, bathed,
      laughing with the waters, and
      saw the sun rise,

4

(8)

III

When I heard at the close of
 the day how I had been
 praised in the Capitol, still
 it was not a happy night
 for me that followed;
Nor when I caroused—
 —Nor when my favorite plans were accom-
 plished—was I really happy.
But that day I rose
 at dawn from the bed of
 perfect health, electric, in-
 haling sweet breath,
When I saw the full moon
 in the west grow pale and
 disappear in the morning light,
When I wandered alone over the
 beach, and undressing, bathed,
 laughing with the waters, and
 saw the sun rise,

And when I thought how
my friend, my lover, was
coming, then I was happy;
O then Each breath tasted
sweeter — and all that day my
food nourished me more — And
the beautiful day passed well,
And the next came with equal
joy — And with the next at
evening, came my friend,

And that night while all
was still, I heard the
waters roll slowly continually
up the shores
I heard the hissing rustle of
the liquid and sands, as directed
to me, whispering to congratulate
me, — For the friend I love lay
sleeping by my side,
In the stillness his face was in-
clined towards me, while the
moon's clear beams shone
And his arm lay lightly over my
breast — And that night I was happy.

And when I thought how
     my friend, my lover, was
     coming, then O I was happy;
Each breath tasted
     sweeter—and all that day my
     food nourished me more—And
     the beautiful day passed well,
And the next came with equal
     joy—And with the next at
     evening, came my friend,
And that night, while all
     was still, I heard the
     waters roll slowly continually
     up the shores
I heard the hissing rustle of
     the liquid and sands, as directed
     to me, whispering, to congratulate
     me,—For the friend I love lay
     sleeping by my side,
In the stillness his face was in-
     clined towards me, while the
     moon's clear beams shone,
And his arm lay lightly over my
     breast—And that night I was happy.

[On this leaf, beneath the paste-over, is an earlier version of the
    conclusion:]
And that night O you happy waters, I heard you beating the shores—
    But my heart beat happier than you—for he I love is returned and
    sleeping by my side,
And that night in the stillness his face was inclined toward me while
    the moon's clear beams shone,
And his arm lay lightly over my breast—And that night I was happy.

IV.

This moment as I sit alone,
yearning and pensive, it
seems to me there are other
men, in other lands, yearning
and pensive.

It seems to me I can look
over and behold them, in
Germany, France, Spain, — Or
far away in China, India,
or Russia — talking other dialects

And it seems to me if I
could know those men better
I should love them as I
love men in my own lands,

It seems to me they are as
wise, beautiful, benevolent,
as any in my own lands;

O I think we should be
brethren — I think I should
be happy with them.

IV

This moment as I sit alone,
        yearning and pensive, it
        seems to me there are other
        men, in other lands, yearning
        and pensive.
It seems to me I can look
        over and behold them, in
        Germany, France, Spain—Or
        far away in China, India or
        Russia—talking other dialects,
And it seems to me if I
        could know those men
        I should love them as I
        love men in my own lands,
It seems to me they are as
        wise, beautiful, benevolent,
        as any in my own lands;
O I think we should be
        brethren—I think I should
        be happy with them.

Long' I thought that knowledge
  alone would suffice me — O
  if I could but obtain
  knowledge,
Then the Land of the Prairies — the south
  Savannas engrossed
engrossed me — me
  For them I would live — I
  would be their orator;
Then I met the examples of old
  and new heroes — I heard the
  examples of warriors, sailors,
  and all dauntless persons —
  And it seemed to me I too
  had it in me to be as
  dauntless as any, and would
  be so;
And then to finish all, it
  came to me to strike up the
  songs of the New World — And
  then I believed my life must
  be spent in singing;
But now take notice, Land of
  the prairies, Land of the south
  Savannas, Ohio's land

V

Long I thought that knowledge
 alone would suffice me — O
 if I could but obtain
 knowledge!
Then the Land of the Prairies engrossed me — the
south savannas engrossed me —
 For them I would live — I
 would be their orator;
Then I met the examples of old
 and new heroes — I heard
 of warriors, sailors,
 and all dauntless persons —
 And it seemed to me I too
 had it in me to be as
 dauntless as any, and would
 be so;
And then to finish all, it
 came to me to strike up the
 songs of the New World — And
 then I believed my life must
 be spent in singing;
But now take notice, Land of
 the prairies, Land of the south
 savannas, Ohio's land,

Take notice, you Kanuck woods
— and you, Lake Huron — and
all that with you roll toward
Niagara — and you Niagara
also,
And you, Californian Mountains—
that you all find some one else
that he be your singer of songs,
For I can be your singer of songs
no longer — I have passed ahead
I have ceased to enjoy them,
I have found him who loves me,
as I him, in perfect love,
With the rest I dispense — I sever
from all that I thought would
suffice me, for it does not — it
is now empty and tasteless
to me,
I heed knowledge, and the grandeur
of The States, and the examples
of heroes, no more,

8

Take notice, you Kanuck woods
      —and you, Lake Huron—and
      all that with you roll toward
      Niagara—and you Niagara
      also,
And you, Californian mountains—
      that you all find some one else
      that he be your singer of songs,
For I can be your singer of songs
      no longer—
      I have ceased to enjoy them.
I have found him who loves me,
      as I him, in perfect love,
With the rest I dispense—I sever
      from all that I thought would
      suffice me, for it does not—it
      is now empty and tasteless
      to me,
I heed knowledge, and the grandeur
      of The States, and the examples
      of heroes, no more,

I am indifferent to my own
songs — I am to go with
him I love, and he is to
go with me,
It is to be enough for each
of us that we are together —
We never separate again.

8½

———~~~———

I am indifferent to my own
        songs—I am to go with
        him I love, and he is to
        go with me,
It is to be enough for each
        of us that we are together—
        We never separate again.—

_____

What think you I have
 taken my pen to record?
Not the battle=ship, perfect=
 model'd majestic, that I saw
 to day arrive in the offing,
 under full sail,
Nor the splendors of the past
 day — nor the splendors of
 the night that envelopes me —
 Nor the glory and growth of
 the great city spread around
 me,

But the two ~~they~~ men I saw
 to=day on the pier, parting
 the parting of dear friends,
The one ~~who~~ to remain hung on
 the other's neck and passionately
 kissed him — while the one
 who ~~departed~~ to depart tightly prest the
 one ~~who~~ to remain in his arms.

VI

What think you I have
      taken my pen to record?
Not the battle-ship, perfect-
      model'd majestic, that I saw
      to day arrive in the offing,
      under full sail,
Nor the splendors of the past
      day—nor the splendors of
      the night that envelopes me—
      Nor the glory and growth of
      the great city spread around
      me,
But the two men I saw
      to-day on the pier, parting
      the parting of dear friends.
The one to remain hung on
      the other's neck and passionately
      kissed him—while the one
      to depart tightly prest the
      one to remain in his arms.

You bards of ages hence! when
    you refer to me, mind not
    so much my poems,
Nor speak of me that I pro-
    phesied of The States and led
    them the way of their glories,
But come, I will inform you
    who I was underneath that
    impassive exterior — I will
    tell you what to say of me,

9½

VII

You bards of ages hence! when
      you refer to me, mind not
      so much my poems,
Nor speak of me that I pro-
      phesied of The States and led
      them the way of their glories,
But come, I will inform you
      who I was underneath that
      impassive exterior—I will
      tell you what to say of me,

Publish my name and hang up
my picture as that of the
tenderest lover,
The friend, the lover's portrait, of
whom his friend, his lover,
was fondest,
Who was not proud of his songs,
but of the measureless ocean
of love within him — and
freely poured it forth,
Who often walked lonesome walks
thinking of his dearest friends,
his lovers,
Who pensive, away from one he
loved, often lay sleepless and
dissatisfied. at night,
Who, dreading lest the one he loved
might after all be indifferent
to him, felt the sick feeling—
O sick! sick!
Whose happiest days were those, far
away, in woods, on hills, he
through fields,
and another wandering hand in
hand, they twain, apart from
other men.

Who ever, as he sauntered the
streets, curved with his arm
the manly shoulder of his
friend — while the curving
arm of his friend rested
upon him also.

10

Publish my name and hang up
    my picture as that of the
    tenderest lover,
The friend, the lover's portrait, of
    whom his friend, his lover,
    was fondest,
Who was not proud of his songs,
    but of the measureless ocean
    of love within him—and
    freely poured it forth,
Who often walked lonesome walks
    thinking of his dearest friends,
    his lovers,
Who pensive, away from one he
    loved, often lay sleepless and
    dissatisfied at night,
Who, dreading lest the one he loved
    might after all be indifferent
    to him, felt the sick feeling—
    O sick! sick!
Whose happiest days were those, far
    away through fields, in woods, on hills, he
    and another, wandering hand in
    hand, they twain, apart from
    other men.
Who ever, as he sauntered the
    streets, curved with his arm
    the manly shoulder of his
    friend—while the curving
    arm of his friend rested
    upon him also.

———————

Hours continuing long, sore
and heavy hearted,
Hours of the dusk, when I
withdraw to a lonesome and
unfrequented spot, seating
myself, leaning my face
in my hands,
Hours sleepless, deep in the night
when I go forth speeding
swiftly the country roads, or
through the city streets, or
pacing miles and miles, stifling
plaintive cries,

81

VIII.
~~IX.~~

Hours continuing long, sore
    and heavy-hearted,
Hours of the dusk, when I
        withdraw to a lonesome and
        unfrequented spot, seating
        myself, leaning my face
        in my hands,
Hours sleepless, deep in the night,
        when I go forth, speeding
        swiftly the country roads, or
        through the city streets, or
        pacing miles and miles, stifling
        plaintive cries,

Hours discouraged, distracted,
— For he, the one I cannot
content myself without —
soon I saw him content
himself without me,
Hours when I am forgotten—
(O weeks and months are
passing, but I believe I am
never to forget!)
Sullen and suffering hours—
(I am ashamed — but it is
useless — I am what I am;)
Hours of my torment — I
wonder if other men ever
have the like, out of the
like feelings?
Is there even one other like
me — distracted — his friend,
his lover, lost to him?
Is he too as I am now? Does
he still rise in the morning,
dejected, thinking who is lost to him?
And at night, awaking, think who is
lost?

Does he too harbor his friendship si:
lent and endless? Harbor his anguish
and passion?
Does some stray reminder, or the
casual mention of a name, bring
the fit back upon him, taciturn
and deprest?
Does he see himself reflected in me?
In these hours does he see the
face of his hours reflected?

12

Hours discouraged, distracted,
       —For he, the one I cannot
       content myself without—
       soon I saw him content
       himself without me,
Hours when I am forgotten—
       (O weeks and months are
       passing, but I believe I am
       never to forget!)
Sullen and suffering hours—
       (I am ashamed—but it is
       useless—I am what I am;)
Hours of my torment—I
       wonder if other men ever
       have the like, out of the
       like feelings?
Is there even one other like
       me—distracted— his friend,
       his lover, lost to him?
Is he too as I am now? Does
       he still rise in the morning,
       dejected, thinking who is lost to him?
       And at night, awaking, think who is
       lost?
Does he too harbor his friendship si-
       lent and endless? Harbor his anguish
       and passion?
Does some stray reminder, or the
       casual mention of a name, bring
       the fit back upon him, taciturn
       and deprest?
Does he see himself reflected in me?
       In these hours does he see the
       face of his hours reflected?

———

I dreamed in a dream of a
  city where all the men
  were like brothers,
O I saw them tenderly love
  each other — I often saw
  them in numbers, walking
  hand in hand;
I dreamed that was the city
  of robust friends — Nothing
  was greater there than the
  quality of manly love — it
  led the rest,
It was seen every hour in the
  actions of the men of that city,
  and in all their looks and
13 words.—

IX

I dreamed in a dream of a
      city where all the men
      were like brothers,
O I saw them tenderly love
      each other—I often saw
      them, in numbers, walking
      hand in hand;
I dreamed that was the city
      of robust friends—Nothing
      was greater there than
      manly love—it
      led the rest,
It was seen every hour in the
      actions of the men of that city,
      and in all their looks and
      words.—

often and

✗

O you whom I silently come
where ⚹ you are, that
I may be with you,
As I walk by your side, or
sit near, or remain in
the same room with you,
Little you know the subtle
electric fire that for
you sake is playing
within me.

14

X

O you whom I often and silently come
   where you are, that
   I may be with you,
As I walk by your side, or
   sit near, or remain in
   the same room with you,
Little you know the subtle
   electric fire that for
   your sake is playing
   within me. —

XII.

Earth! My likeness! Though
    you look so impassive,
    ample and spheric there,
    — I now suspect that
    is not all,
I now suspect there is
    something terrible in you,
    ready to break forth,
For an athlete loves me,
    and I him — But toward
    him there is something
    fierce and terrible in me,
I dare not tell it in words—
    not even in these songs.

15

(34)

XI

Earth! Though
       you look so impassive,
       ample and spheric there
       —I now suspect that
       is not all,
I now suspect there is
       something terrible in you,
       ready to break forth,
For an athlete loves me,
       and I him—But toward
       him there is something
       fierce and terrible in me,
I dare not tell it in words—
       not even in these songs.

XII Calamus 42
p. 377

To the young man, many
things to absorb, to engraft,
to develope, I teach, that
he be my eleve,
But if through him rolls
not the red blood of
divine friendship, hot
and red — If he be not
silently selected by lovers,
and do not silently select
lovers — of what use were
it for him to seek to
become eleve of mine?

16

XII

To the young man, many
        things to absorb, to engraft,
        to develop, I teach, that
        he be my eleve,
But if through him speed
        not the blood of
        friendship, hot
        and red—If he be not
        silently selected by lovers,
        and do not silently select
        lovers—of what use were
        it for him to seek to
        become eleve of mine?

Calamus, 1860

CALAMUS.

1.

In paths untrodden,
In the growth by margins of pond-waters,
Escaped from the life that exhibits itself,
From all the standards hitherto published — from
    the pleasures, profits, conformities,
Which too long I was offering to feed to my Soul;
Clear to me now, standards not yet published —
    clear to me that my Soul,
That the Soul of the man I speak for, feeds, rejoices
    only in comrades;
Here, by myself, away from the clank of the world,
Tallying and talked to here by tongues aromatic,
No longer abashed — for in this secluded spot I can
    respond as I would not dare elsewhere,
Strong upon me the life that does not exhibit itself,
    yet contains all the rest,
Resolved to sing no songs to-day but those of manly
    attachment,
Projecting them along that substantial life,
Bequeathing, hence, types of athletic love,

Afternoon, this delicious Ninth Month, in my forty-
first year,
I proceed, for all who are, or have been, young
men,
To tell the secret of my nights and days,
To celebrate the need of comrades.

2.

Scented herbage of my breast,
Leaves from you I yield, I write, to be perused best
afterwards,
Tomb-leaves, body-leaves, growing up above me, above
death,
Perennial roots, tall leaves — O the winter shall not
freeze you, delicate leaves,
Every year shall you bloom again — Out from where
you retired, you shall emerge again ;
O I do not know whether many, passing by, will dis-
cover you, or inhale your faint odor — but I
believe a few will ;
O slender leaves ! O blossoms of my blood ! I permit
you to tell, in your own way, of the heart that is
under you,
O burning and throbbing — surely all will one day be
accomplished ;
O I do not know what you mean, there underneath
yourselves — you are not happiness,
You are often more bitter than I can bear — you burn
and sting me,

Yet you are very beautiful to me, you faint-tinged
    roots — you make me think of Death,
Death is beautiful from you — (what indeed is beau-
    tiful, except Death and Love ?)
O I think it is not for life I am chanting here my
    chant of lovers — I think it must be for Death,
For how calm, how solemn it grows, to ascend to the
    atmosphere of lovers,
Death or life I am then indifferent — my Soul de-
    clines to prefer,
I am not sure but the high Soul of lovers welcomes
    death most ;
Indeed, O Death, I think now these leaves mean pre-
    cisely the same as you mean ;
Grow up taller, sweet leaves, that I may see ! Grow
    up out of my breast !
Spring away from the concealed heart there !
Do not fold yourselves so in your pink-tinged roots,
    timid leaves !
Do not remain down there so ashamed, herbage of my
    breast !
Come, I am determined to unbare this broad breast of
    mine — I have long enough stifled and choked ;
Emblematic and capricious blades, I leave you — now
    you serve me not,
Away ! I will say what I have to say, by itself,
I will escape from the sham that was proposed to me,
I will sound myself and comrades only — I will never
    again utter a call, only their call,
I will raise, with it, immortal reverberations through
    The States,
I will give an example to lovers, to take permanent
    shape and will through The States ;

Through me shall the words be said to make death
    exhilarating,
Give me your tone therefore, O Death, that I may
    accord with it,
Give me yourself — for I see that you belong to me
    now above all, and are folded together above all
    — you Love and Death are,
Nor will I allow you to balk me any more with what
    I was calling life,
For now it is conveyed to me that you are the pur-
    ports essential,
That you hide in these shifting forms of life, for
    reasons — and that they are mainly for you,
That you, beyond them, come forth, to remain, the
    real reality,
That behind the mask of materials you patiently
    wait, no matter how long,
That you will one day, perhaps, take control of all,
That you will perhaps dissipate this entire show of
    appearance,
That may be you are what it is all for — but it does
    not last so very long,
But you will last very long.

3.

1. WHOEVER you are holding me now in hand,
Without one thing all will be useless,
I give you fair warning, before you attempt me
    further,
I am not what you supposed, but far different.

2. Who is he that would become my follower?
   Who would sign himself a candidate for my affec-
      tions? Are you he?

3. The way is suspicious — the result slow, uncertain,
      may-be destructive;
   You would have to give up all else — I alone would
      expect to be your God, sole and exclusive,
   Your novitiate would even then be long and ex-
      hausting,
   The whole past theory of your life, and all conformity
      to the lives around you, would have to be aban-
      doned;
   Therefore release me now, before troubling yourself
      any further — Let go your hand from my
      shoulders,
   Put me down, and depart on your way.

4. Or else, only by stealth, in some wood, for trial,
   Or back of a rock, in the open air,
   (For in any roofed room of a house I emerge not —
      nor in company,
   And in libraries I lie as one dumb, a gawk, or unborn,
      or dead,)
   But just possibly with you on a high hill — first
      watching lest any person, for miles around,
      approach unawares,
   Or possibly with you sailing at sea, or on the beach of
      the sea, or some quiet island,
   Here to put your lips upon mine I permit you,
   With the comrade's long-dwelling kiss, or the new
      husband's kiss,
   For I am the new husband, and I am the comrade.

5. Or, if you will, thrusting me beneath your clothing,
   Where I may feel the throbs of your heart, or rest
        upon your hip,
   Carry me when you go forth over land or sea ;
   For thus, merely touching you, is enough — is best,
   And thus, touching you, would I silently sleep and be
        carried eternally.

6. But these leaves conning, you con at peril,
   For these leaves, and me, you will not understand,
   They will elude you at first, and still more after-
        ward — I will certainly elude you,
   Even while you should think you had unquestionably
        caught me, behold !
   Already you see I have escaped from you.

7. For it is not for what I have put into it that I have
        written this book,
   Nor is it by reading it you will acquire it,
   Nor do those know me best who admire me, and
        vauntingly praise me,
   Nor will the candidates for my love, (unless at most a
        very few,) prove victorious,
   Nor will my poems do good only — they will do just
        as much evil, perhaps more,
   For all is useless without that which you may guess
        at many times and not hit — that which I
        hinted at,
   Therefore release me, and depart on your way.

4.

These I, singing in spring, collect for lovers,
(For who but I should understand lovers, and all their
 sorrow and joy ?
And who but I should be the poet of comrades ?)
Collecting, I traverse the garden, the world — but
 soon I pass the gates,
Now along the pond-side — now wading in a little,
 fearing not the wet,
Now by the post-and-rail fences, where the old stones
 thrown there, picked from the fields, have accu-
 mulated,
Wild-flowers and vines and weeds come up through
 the stones, and partly cover them — Beyond these
 I pass,
Far, far in the forest, before I think where I get,
Solitary, smelling the earthy smell, stopping now and
 then in the silence,
Alone I had thought — yet soon a silent troop gathers
 around me,
Some walk by my side, and some behind, and some
 embrace my arms or neck,
They, the spirits of friends, dead or alive — thicker
 they come, a great crowd, and I in the middle,
Collecting, dispensing, singing in spring, there I wan-
 der with them,
Plucking something for tokens — something for these,
 till I hit upon a name — tossing toward whoever
 is near me,

Here ! lilac, with a branch of pine,

Here, out of my pocket, some moss which I pulled off
   a live-oak in Florida, as it hung trailing down,

Here, some pinks and laurel leaves, and a handful of
   sage,

And here what I now draw from the water, wading in
   the pond-side,

(O here I last saw him that tenderly loves me — and
   returns again, never to separate from me,

And this, O this shall henceforth be the token of
   comrades — this calamus-root shall,

Interchange it, youths, with each other! Let none
   render it back!)

And twigs of maple, and a bunch of wild orange, and
   chestnut,

And stems of currants, and plum-blows, and the
   aromatic cedar ;

These I, compassed around by a thick cloud of
   spirits,

Wandering, point to, or touch as I pass, or throw them
   loosely from me,

Indicating to each one what he shall have — giving
   something to each,

But what I drew from the water by the pond-side, that
   I reserve,

I will give of it — but only to them that love, as I
   myself am capable of loving.

5.

1. STATES!
  Were you looking to be held together by the lawyers?
  By an agreement on a paper? Or by arms?

2. Away!
  I arrive, bringing these, beyond all the forces of
    courts and arms,
  These! to hold you together as firmly as the earth
    itself is held together.

3. The old breath of life, ever new,
  Here! I pass it by contact to you, America.

4. O mother! have you done much for me?
  Behold, there shall from me be much done for you.

5. There shall from me be a new friendship — It shall
    be called after my name,
  It shall circulate through The States, indifferent of
    place,
  It shall twist and intertwist them through and around
    each other — Compact shall they be, showing
    new signs,
  Affection shall solve every one of the problems of
    freedom,
  Those who love each other shall be invincible,
  They shall finally make America completely victo-
    rious, in my name.

30

6. One from Massachusetts shall be comrade to a Missourian,
   One from Maine or Vermont, and a Carolinian and an Oregonese, shall be friends triune, more precious to each other than all the riches of the earth.

7. To Michigan shall be wafted perfume from Florida,
   To the Mannahatta from Cuba or Mexico,
   Not the perfume of flowers, but sweeter, and wafted beyond death.

8. No danger shall balk Columbia's lovers,
   If need be, a thousand shall sternly immolate themselves for one,
   The Kanuck shall be willing to lay down his life for the Kansian, and the Kansian for the Kanuck, on due need.

9. It shall be customary in all directions, in the houses and streets, to see manly affection,
   The departing brother or friend shall salute the remaining brother or friend with a kiss.

10. There shall be innovations,
    There shall be countless linked hands — namely, the Northeasterner's, and the Northwesterner's, and the Southwesterner's, and those of the interior, and all their brood,
    These shall be masters of the world under a new power,
    They shall laugh to scorn the attacks of all the remainder of the world.

11. The most dauntless and rude shall touch face to face
lightly,
The dependence of Liberty shall be lovers,
The continuance of Equality shall be comrades.

12. These shall tie and band stronger than hoops of iron,
I, extatic, O partners! O lands! henceforth with the
love of lovers tie you.

13. I will make the continent indissoluble,
I will make the most splendid race the sun ever yet
shone upon,
I will make divine magnetic lands.

14. I will plant companionship thick as trees along all the
rivers of America, and along the shores of the
great lakes, and all over the prairies,
I will make inseparable cities, with their arms about
each other's necks.

15. For you these, from me, O Democracy, to serve you,
ma femme!
For you! for you, I am trilling these songs.

Not heaving from my ribbed breast only,
Not in sighs at night, in rage, dissatisfied with myself,
Not in those long-drawn, ill-suppressed sighs,
Not in many an oath and promise broken,
Not in my wilful and savage soul's volition,

Not in the subtle nourishment of the air,

Not in this beating and pounding at my temples and
wrists,

Not in the curious systole and diastole within, which
will one day cease,

Not in many a hungry wish, told to the skies only,

Not in cries, laughter, defiances, thrown from me
when alone, far in the wilds,

Not in husky pantings through clenched teeth,

Not in sounded and resounded words — chattering
words, echoes, dead words,

Not in the murmurs of my dreams while I sleep,

Nor the other murmurs of these incredible dreams of
every day,

Nor in the limbs and senses of my body, that take you
and dismiss you continually — Not there,

Not in any or all of them, O adhesiveness! O pulse
of my life!

Need I that you exist and show yourself, any more
than in these songs.

7.

OF the terrible question of appearances,

Of the doubts, the uncertainties after all,

That may-be reliance and hope are but speculations
after all,

That may-be identity beyond the grave is a beautiful
fable only,

May-be the things I perceive — the animals, plants,
men, hills, shining and flowing waters,

The skies of day and night — colors, densities, forms
— May-be these are, (as doubtless they are,) only
apparitions, and the real something has yet to be
known,
(How often they dart out of themselves, as if to con-
found me and mock me!
How often I think neither I know, nor any man
knows, aught of them;)
May-be they only seem to me what they are, (as
doubtless they indeed but seem,) as from my
present point of view — And might prove, (as of
course they would,) naught of what they appear,
or naught any how, from entirely changed points
of view;
To me, these, and the like of these, are curiously
answered by my lovers, my dear friends;
When he whom I love travels with me, or sits a long
while holding me by the hand,
When the subtle air, the impalpable, the sense that
words and reason hold not, surround us and
pervade us,
Then I am charged with untold and untellable wis-
dom — I am silent — I require nothing further,
I cannot answer the question of appearances, or that
of identity beyond the grave,
But I walk or sit indifferent — I am satisfied,
He ahold of my hand has completely satisfied me.

8.

LONG I thought that knowledge alone would suffice
me — O if I could but obtain knowledge!

Then my lands engrossed me — Lands of the prairies,
Ohio's land, the southern savannas, engrossed
me — For them I would live — I would be their
orator;

Then I met the examples of old and new heroes — I
heard of warriors, sailors, and all dauntless per-
sons — And it seemed to me that I too had it
in me to be as dauntless as any — and would
be so;

And then, to enclose all, it came to me to strike up
the songs of the New World — And then I be-
lieved my life must be spent in singing;

But now take notice, land of the prairies, land of
the south savannas, Ohio's land,

Take notice, you Kanuck woods — and you Lake
Huron — and all that with you roll toward
Niagara — and you Niagara also,

And you, Californian mountains — That you each
and all find somebody else to be your singer of
songs,

For I can be your singer of songs no longer — One
who loves me is jealous of me, and withdraws me
from all but love,

With the rest I dispense — I sever from what I
thought would suffice me, for it does not — it is
now empty and tasteless to me,

I heed knowledge, and the grandeur of The States,
and the example of heroes, no more,

I am indifferent to my own songs — I will go with
    him I love,
It is to be enough for us that we are together — We
    never separate again.

9.

HOURS continuing long, sore and heavy-hearted,
Hours of the dusk, when I withdraw to a lonesome
    and unfrequented spot, seating myself, leaning
    my face in my hands;
Hours sleepless, deep in the night, when I go forth,
    speeding swiftly the country roads, or through
    the city streets, or pacing miles and miles, sti-
    fling plaintive cries;
Hours discouraged, distracted — for the one I cannot
    content myself without, soon I saw him content
    himself without me;
Hours when I am forgotten, (O weeks and months are
    passing, but I believe I am never to forget!)
Sullen and suffering hours! (I am ashamed — but it
    is useless — I am what I am;)
Hours of my torment — I wonder if other men ever
    have the like, out of the like feelings?
Is there even one other like me — distracted — his
    friend, his lover, lost to him?
Is he too as I am now? Does he still rise in the morn-
    ing, dejected, thinking who is lost to him? and
    at night, awaking, think who is lost?

Does he too harbor his friendship silent and endless ? harbor his anguish and passion ?

Does some stray reminder, or the casual mention of a name, bring the fit back upon him, taciturn and deprest ?

Does he see himself reflected in me ? In these hours, does he see the face of his hours reflected ?

10.

You bards of ages hence ! when you refer to me, mind not so much my poems,

Nor speak of me that I prophesied of The States, and led them the way of their glories ;

But come, I will take you down underneath this impassive exterior — I will tell you what to say of me :

Publish my name and hang up my picture as that of the tenderest lover,

The friend, the lover's portrait, of whom his friend, his lover, was fondest,

Who was not proud of his songs, but of the measureless ocean of love within him — and freely poured it forth,

Who often walked lonesome walks, thinking of his dear friends, his lovers,

Who pensive, away from one he loved, often lay sleepless and dissatisfied at night,

Who knew too well the sick, sick dread lest the one he loved might secretly be indifferent to him,

Whose happiest days were far away, through fields, in
    woods, on hills, he and another, wandering hand
    in hand, they twain, apart from other men,
Who oft as he sauntered the streets, curved with his
    arm the shoulder of his friend — while the arm of
    his friend rested upon him also.

11.

WHEN I heard at the close of the day how my name
    had been received with plaudits in the capitol,
    still it was not a happy night for me that fol-
    lowed ;
And else, when I caroused, or when my plans were
    accomplished, still I was not happy ;
But the day when I rose at dawn from the bed of
    perfect health, refreshed, singing, inhaling the
    ripe breath of autumn,
When I saw the full moon in the west grow pale and
    disappear in the morning light,
When I wandered alone over the beach, and, undress-
    ing, bathed, laughing with the cool waters, and
    saw the sun rise,
And when I thought how my dear friend, my lover,
    was on his way coming, O then I was happy ;
O then each breath tasted sweeter — and all that day
    my food nourished me more — And the beautiful
    day passed well,
And the next came with equal joy — And with the
    next, at evening, came my friend ;

And that night, while all was still, I heard the waters
    roll slowly continually up the shores,
I heard the hissing rustle of the liquid and sands,
    as directed to me, whispering, to congratulate
    me,
For the one I love most lay sleeping by me under the
    same cover in the cool night,
In the stillness, in the autumn moonbeams, his face
    was inclined toward me,
And his arm lay lightly around my breast — And that
    night I was happy.

12.

Are you the new person drawn toward me, and asking
    something significant from me ?
To begin with, take warning — I am probably far
    different from what you suppose ;
Do you suppose you will find in me your ideal ?
Do you think it so easy to have me become your
    lover ?
Do you think the friendship of me would be unalloyed
    satisfaction ?
Do you suppose I am trusty and faithful ?
Do you see no further than this façade — this smooth
    and tolerant manner of me ?
Do you suppose yourself advancing on real ground
    toward a real heroic man ?
Have you no thought, O dreamer, that it may be all
    maya, illusion ?   O the next step may precipitate
    you !

O let some past deceived one hiss in your ears, how
many have prest on the same as you are pressing
now,

How many have fondly supposed what you are sup-
posing now — only to be disappointed.

13.

Calamus taste,

(For I must change the strain — these are not to be
pensive leaves, but leaves of joy,)

Roots and leaves unlike any but themselves,

Scents brought to men and women from the wild
woods, and from the pond-side,

Breast-sorrel and pinks of love — fingers that wind
around tighter than vines,

Gushes from the throats of birds, hid in the foliage
of trees, as the sun is risen,

Breezes of land and love — Breezes set from living
shores out to you on the living sea — to you,
O sailors !

Frost-mellowed berries, and Third Month twigs, of-
fered fresh to young persons wandering out in
the fields when the winter breaks up,

Love-buds, put before you and within you, whoever
you are,

Buds to be unfolded on the old terms,

If you bring the warmth of the sun to them, they will
open, and bring form, color, perfume, to you,

If you become the aliment and the wet, they will
become flowers, fruits, tall branches and trees,

They are comprised in you just as much as in them-
    selves — perhaps more than in themselves,
They are not comprised in one season or succession,
    but many successions,
They have come slowly up out of the earth and me,
    and are to come slowly up out of you.

14.

NOT heat flames up and consumes,
Not sea-waves hurry in and out,
Not the air, delicious and dry, the air of the ripe
    summer, bears lightly along white down-balls of
    myriads of seeds, wafted, sailing gracefully, to
    drop where they may,
Not these — O none of these, more than the flames
    of me, consuming, burning for his love whom I
    love !
O none, more than I, hurrying in and out;
Does the tide hurry, seeking something, and never
    give up ? O I the same ;
O nor down-balls, nor perfumes, nor the high
    rain-emitting clouds, are borne through the open
    air,
Any more than my Soul is borne through the open
    air,
Wafted in all directions, O love, for friendship, for
    you.

15.

O DROPS of me! trickle, slow drops,
Candid, from me falling — drip, bleeding drops,
From wounds made to free you whence you were
prisoned,
From my face — from my forehead and lips,
From my breast — from within where I was con-
cealed — Press forth, red drops — confession
drops,
Stain every page — stain every song I sing, every
word I say, bloody drops,
Let them know your scarlet heat — let them glisten,
Saturate them with yourself, all ashamed and wet,
Glow upon all I have written or shall write, bleed-
ing drops,
Let it all be seen in your light, blushing drops.

16.

1. WHO is now reading this?

2. May-be one is now reading this who knows some
wrong-doing of my past life,
Or may-be a stranger is reading this who has secretly
loved me,
Or may-be one who meets all my grand assumptions
and egotisms with derision,
Or may-be one who is puzzled at me.

31

3. As if I were not puzzled at myself!

Or as if I never deride myself! (O conscience-struck!
O self-convicted!)

Or as if I do not secretly love strangers! (O tenderly,
a long time, and never avow it;)

Or as if I did not see, perfectly well, interior in
myself, the stuff of wrong-doing,

Or as if it could cease transpiring from me until it
must cease.

17.

Of him I love day and night, I dreamed I heard he
was dead,

And I dreamed I went where they had buried him I
love — but he was not in that place,

And I dreamed I wandered, searching among burial-
places, to find him,

And I found that every place was a burial-place,

The houses full of life were equally full of death,
(This house is now,)

The streets, the shipping, the places of amusement,
the Chicago, Boston, Philadelphia, the Manna-
hatta, were as full of the dead as of the living,

And fuller, O vastly fuller, of the dead than of the
living;

— And what I dreamed I will henceforth tell to every
person and age,

And I stand henceforth bound to what I dreamed;

And now I am willing to disregard burial-places, and
dispense with them,

And if the memorials of the dead were put up indif-
ferently everywhere, even in the room where I
eat or sleep, I should be satisfied,
And if the corpse of any one I love, or if my own
corpse, be duly rendered to powder, and poured
in the sea, I shall be satisfied,
Or if it be distributed to the winds, I shall be sat-
isfied.

18.

City of my walks and joys !
City whom that I have lived and sung there will one
day make you illustrious,
Not the pageants of you — not your shifting tab-
leaux, your spectacles, repay me,
Not the interminable rows of your houses — nor the
ships at the wharves,
Nor the processions in the streets, nor the bright win-
dows, with goods in them,
Nor to converse with learned persons, or bear my
share in the soiree or feast;
Not those — but, as I pass, O Manhattan ! your fre-
quent and swift flash of eyes offering me love,
Offering me the response of my own — these repay
me,
Lovers, continual lovers, only repay me.

19.

1. Mind you the the timid models of the rest, the majority?
Long I minded them, but hence I will not — for I have adopted models for myself, and now offer them to The Lands.

2. Behold this swarthy and unrefined face — these gray eyes,
This beard — the white wool, unclipt upon my neck,
My brown hands, and the silent manner of me, without charm;
Yet comes one, a Manhattanese, and ever at parting, kisses me lightly on the lips with robust love,
And I, in the public room, or on the crossing of the street, or on the ship's deck, kiss him in return;
We observe that salute of American comrades, land and sea,
We are those two natural and nonchalant persons.

20.

I saw in Louisiana a live-oak growing,
All alone stood it, and the moss hung down from the branches,
Without any companion it grew there, uttering joyous leaves of dark green,
And its look, rude, unbending, lusty, made me think of myself,

But I wondered how it could utter joyous leaves,
  standing alone there, without its friend, its
  lover near — for I knew I could not,
And I broke off a twig with a certain number of
  leaves upon it, and twined around it a little
  moss,
And brought it away — and I have placed it in sight
  in my room,
It is not needed to remind me as of my own dear
  friends,
(For I believe lately I think of little else than of
  them,)
Yet it remains to me a curious token — it makes me
  think of manly love ;
For all that, and though the live-oak glistens there in
  Louisiana, solitary, in a wide flat space,
Uttering joyous leaves all its life, without a friend, a
  lover, near,
I know very well I could not.

21.

Music always round me, unceasing, unbeginning —
  yet long untaught I did not hear,
But now the chorus I hear, and am elated,
A tenor, strong, ascending, with power and health,
  with glad notes of day-break I hear,
A soprano, at intervals, sailing buoyantly over the
  tops of immense waves,
A transparent base, shuddering lusciously under and
  through the universe,

31*

(65)

The triumphant tutti — the funeral wailings, with sweet flutes and violins — All these I fill myself with ;

I hear not the volumes of sound merely — I am moved by the exquisite meanings,

I listen to the different voices winding in and out, striving, contending with fiery vehemence to excel each other in emotion,

I do not think the performers know themselves — But now I think I begin to know them.

22.

Passing stranger ! you do not know how longingly I look upon you,

You must be he I was seeking, or she I was seeking, (It comes to me, as of a dream,)

I have somewhere surely lived a life of joy with you,

All is recalled as we flit by each other, fluid, affectionate, chaste, matured,

You grew up with me, were a boy with me, or a girl with me,

I ate with you, and slept with you — your body has become not yours only, nor left my body mine only,

You give me the pleasure of your eyes, face, flesh, as we pass — you take of my beard, breast, hands, in return,

I am not to speak to you — I am to think of you when I sit alone, or wake at night alone,

I am to wait — I do not doubt I am to meet you
    again,
I am to see to it that I do not lose you.

23.

THIS moment as I sit alone, yearning and thoughtful,
    it seems to me there are other men in other
    lands, yearning and thoughtful;
It seems to me I can look over and behold them,
    in Germany, Italy, France, Spain — Or far, far
    away, in China, or in Russia or India — talking
    other dialects;
And it seems to me if I could know those men better,
    I should become attached to them, as I do to men
    in my own lands,
It seems to me they are as wise, beautiful, benevolent,
    as any in my own lands;
O I know we should be brethren and lovers,
I know I should be happy with them.

24.

I HEAR it is charged against me that I seek to destroy
    institutions;
But really I am neither for nor against institutions,
(What indeed have I in common with them ? — Or
    what with the destruction of them ?)

Only I will establish in the Mannahatta, and in every
city of These States, inland and seaboard,
And in the fields and woods, and above every kęel
little or large, that dents the water,
Without edifices, or rules, or trustees, or any ar-
gument,
The institution of the dear love of comrades.

25.

The prairie-grass dividing — its own odor breathing,
I demand of it the spiritual corresponding,
Demand the most copious and close companionship
of men,
Demand the blades to rise of words, acts, beings,
Those of the open atmosphere, coarse, sunlit, fresh,
nutritious,
Those that go their own gait, erect, stepping with
freedom and command — leading, not following,
Those with a never-quell'd audacity — those with
sweet and lusty flesh, clear of taint, choice and
chary of its love-power,
Those that look carelessly in the faces of Presidents
and Governors, as to say, *Who are you?*
Those of earth-born passion, simple, never constrained,
never obedient,
Those of inland America.

26.

WE two boys together clinging,
One the other never leaving,
Up and down the roads going — North and South
excursions making,
Power enjoying — elbows stretching — fingers clutch-
ing,
Armed and fearless — eating, drinking, sleeping, lov-
ing,
No law less than ourselves owning — sailing, soldier-
ing, thieving, threatening,
Misers, menials, priests alarming — air breathing,
water drinking, on the turf or the sea-beach
dancing,
With birds singing — With fishes swimming — With
trees branching and leafing,
Cities wrenching, ease scorning, statutes mocking,
feebleness chasing,
Fulfilling our foray.

27.

O LOVE!
O dying — always dying!
O the burials of me, past and present!
O me, while I stride ahead, material, visible, imperi-
ous as ever!

O me, what I was for years, now dead, (I lament not
    — I am content;)
O to disengage myself from those corpses of me,
    which I turn and look at, where I cast them!
To pass on, (O living! always living!) and leave the
    corpses behind!

28.

WHEN I peruse the conquered fame of heroes, and the
    victories of mighty generals, I do not envy the
    generals,
Nor the President in his Presidency, nor the rich in
    his great house;
But when I read of the brotherhood of lovers, how it
    was with them,
How through life, through dangers, odium, un-
    changing, long and long,
Through youth, and through middle and old age, how
    unfaltering, how affectionate and faithful they
    were,
Then I am pensive — I hastily put down the book,
    and walk away, filled with the bitterest envy.

29.

ONE flitting glimpse, caught through an interstice,
Of a crowd of workmen and drivers in a bar-room,
    around the stove, late of a winter night — And
    I unremarked, seated in a corner ;
Of a youth who loves me, and whom I love, silently
    approaching, and seating himself near, that he
    may hold me by the hand ;
A long while, amid the noises of coming and going
    — of drinking and oath and smutty jest,
There we two, content, happy in being together,
    speaking little, perhaps not a word.

30.

A PROMISE and gift to California,
Also to the great Pastoral Plains, and for Oregon :
Sojourning east a while longer, soon I travel to you,
    to remain, to teach robust American love ;
For I know very well that I and robust love belong
    among you, inland, and along the Western
    Sea,
For These States tend inland, and toward the Western
    Sea — and I will also.

31.

1. WHAT ship, puzzled at sea, cons for the true reck-
oning ?
Or, coming in, to avoid the bars, and follow the chan-
nel, a perfect pilot needs ?
Here, sailor ! Here, ship ! take aboard the most per-
fect pilot,
Whom, in a little boat, putting off, and rowing, I,
hailing you, offer.

2. What place is besieged, and vainly tries to raise the
siege ?
Lo ! I send to that place a commander, swift, brave,
immortal,
And with him horse and foot — and parks of artillery,
And artillerymen, the deadliest that ever fired gun.

32.

WHAT think you I take my pen in hand to record ?
The battle-ship, perfect-model'd, majestic, that I saw
pass the offing to-day under full sail ?
The splendors of the past day ? Or the splendor of the
night that envelops me ?
Or the vaunted glory and growth of the great city
spread around me ? — No ;
But I record of two simple men I saw to-day, on the
pier, in the midst of the crowd, parting the part-
ing of dear friends,

The one to remain hung on the other's neck, and pas-
sionately kissed him,
While the one to depart, tightly prest the one to
remain in his arms.

33.

No labor-saving machine,
Nor discovery have I made,
Nor will I be able to leave behind me any wealthy
bequest to found a hospital or library,
Nor reminiscence of any deed of courage, for America,
Nor literary success, nor intellect — nor book for the
book-shelf;
Only these carols, vibrating through the air, I leave,
For comrades and lovers.

34.

I DREAMED in a dream, I saw a city invincible to the
attacks of the whole of the rest of the earth,
I dreamed that was the new City of Friends,
Nothing was greater there than the quality of robust
love — it led the rest,
It was seen every hour in the actions of the men of
that city,
And in all their looks and words.

32

35.

To you of New England,
To the man of the Seaside State, and of Pennsylvania,
To the Kanadian of the north — to the Southerner I
    love,
These, with perfect trust, to depict you as myself —
    the germs are in all men ;
I believe the main purport of These States is to found
    a superb friendship, exalté, previously unknown,
Because I perceive it waits, and has been always wait-
    ing, latent in all men.

36.

EARTH ! my likeness !
Though you look so impassive, ample and spheric
    there,
I now suspect that is not all ;
I now suspect there is something fierce in you, eligible
    to burst forth ;
For an athlete is enamoured of me — and I of him,
But toward him there is something fierce and terrible
    in me, eligible to burst forth,
I dare not tell it in words — not even in these songs.

37.

A Leaf for hand in hand!
You natural persons old and young! You on the
Eastern Sea, and you on the Western!
You on the Mississippi, and on all the branches and
bayous of the Mississippi!
You friendly boatmen and mechanics! You roughs!
You twain! And all processions moving along the
streets!
I wish to infuse myself among you till I see it com-
mon for you to walk hand in hand.

38.

PRIMEVAL my love for the woman I love,
O bride! O wife! more resistless, more enduring
than I can tell, the thought of you!
Then separate, as disembodied, the purest born,
The ethereal, the last athletic reality, my consolation,
I ascend — I float in the regions of your love, O man,
O sharer of my roving life.

39.

SOMETIMES with one I love, I fill myself with rage, for
fear I effuse unreturned love;
But now I think there is no unreturned love — the
pay is certain, one way or another,

Doubtless I could not have perceived the universe,
　　or written one of my poems, if I had not freely
　　given myself to comrades, to love.

40.

That shadow, my likeness, that goes to and fro, seek-
　　ing a livelihood, chattering, chaffering,
How often I find myself standing and looking at it
　　where it flits,
How often I question and doubt whether that is really
　　me ;
But in these, and among my lovers, and carolling my
　　songs,
O I never doubt whether that is really me.

41.

1. Among the men and women, the multitude, I per-
　　ceive one picking me out by secret and divine
　　signs,
　　Acknowledging none else — not parent, wife, hus-
　　band, brother, child, any nearer than I am ;
　　Some are baffled — But that one is not — that one
　　knows me.

2. Lover and perfect equal !
　　I meant that you should discover me so, by my faint
　　indirections,
　　And I, when I meet you, mean to discover you by the
　　like in you.

42.

To the young man, many things to absorb, to engraft,
to develop, I teach, to help him become élève of
mine,
But if blood like mine circle not in his veins,
If he be not silently selected by lovers, and do not
silently select lovers,
Of what use is it that he seek to become élève of
mine ?

43.

O you whom I often and silently come where you
are, that I may be with you,
As I walk by your side, or sit near, or remain in the
same room with you,
Little you know the subtle electric fire that for your
sake is playing within me.

44.

Here my last words, and the most baffling,
Here the frailest leaves of me, and yet my strongest-
lasting,
Here I shade down and hide my thoughts — I do not
expose them,
And yet they expose me more than all my other
poems.

32 *

45.

1. FULL of life, sweet-blooded, compact, visible,
   I, forty years old the Eighty-third Year of The States,
   To one a century hence, or any number of centuries
   hence,
   To you, yet unborn, these, seeking you.

2. When you read these, I, that was visible, am become
   invisible;
   Now it is you, compact, visible, realizing my poems,
   seeking me,
   Fancying how happy you were, if I could be with
   you, and become your lover;
   Be it as if I were with you. Be not too certain but I
   am now with you.

Calamus, 1881

FACING WEST FROM CALIFORNIA'S SHORES.

FACING west from California's shores,
Inquiring, tireless, seeking what is yet unfound,
I, a child, very old, over waves, towards the house of maternity,
 the land of migrations, look afar,
Look off the shores of my Western sea, the circle almost circled ;
For starting westward from Hindustan, from the vales of Kash-
 mere,
From Asia, from the north, from the God, the sage, and the
 hero,
From the south, from the flowery peninsulas and the spice islands,
Long having wander'd since, round the earth having wander'd,
Now I face home again, very pleas'd and joyous,
(But where is what I started for so long ago?
And why is it yet unfound?)

AS ADAM EARLY IN THE MORNING.

As Adam early in the morning,
Walking forth from the bower refresh'd with sleep,
Behold me where I pass, hear my voice, approach,
Touch me, touch the palm of your hand to my body as I pass,
Be not afraid of my body.

CALAMUS.

IN PATHS UNTRODDEN.

IN paths untrodden,
In the growth by margins of pond-waters,
Escaped from the life that exhibits itself,
From all the standards hitherto publish'd, from the pleasures,
 profits, conformities,
Which too long I was offering to feed my soul,
Clear to me now standards not yet publish'd, clear to me that my
 soul,
That the soul of the man I speak for rejoices in comrades,
Here by myself away from the clank of the world,
Tallying and talk'd to here by tongues aromatic,

No longer abash'd, (for in this secluded spot I can respond as I
　　　　would not dare elsewhere,)
Strong upon me the life that does not exhibit itself, yet contains
　　　　all the rest,
Resolv'd to sing no songs to-day but those of manly attachment,
Projecting them along that substantial life,
Bequeathing hence types of athletic love,
Afternoon this delicious Ninth-month in my forty-first year,
I proceed for all who are or have been young men,
To tell the secret of my nights and days,
To celebrate the need of comrades.

SCENTED HERBAGE OF MY BREAST.

SCENTED herbage of my breast,
Leaves from you I glean, I write, to be perused best afterwards,
Tomb-leaves, body-leaves growing up above me above death,
Perennial roots, tall leaves, O the winter shall not freeze you
　　　　delicate leaves,
Every year shall you bloom again, out from where you retired you
　　　　shall emerge again ;
O I do not know whether many passing by will discover you or
　　　　inhale your faint odor, but I believe a few will ;
O slender leaves ! O blossoms of my blood ! I permit you to tell
　　　　in your own way of the heart that is under you,
O I do not know what you mean there underneath yourselves, you
　　　　are not happiness,
You are often more bitter than I can bear, you burn and sting me,
Yet you are beautiful to me you faint tinged roots, you make me
　　　　think of death,
Death is beautiful from you, (what indeed is finally beautiful except
　　　　death and love ?)
O I think it is not for life I am chanting here my chant of lovers,
　　　　I think it must be for death,
For how calm, how solemn it grows to ascend to the atmosphere
　　　　of lovers,
Death or life I am then indifferent, my soul declines to prefer,
(I am not sure but the high soul of lovers welcomes death most,)
Indeed O death, I think now these leaves mean precisely the same
　　　　as you mean,
Grow up taller sweet leaves that I may see ! grow up out of my
　　　　breast !
Spring away from the conceal'd heart there !
Do not fold yourself so in your pink-tinged roots timid leaves !

Do not remain down there so ashamed, herbage of my breast !
Come I am determin'd to unbare this broad breast of mine, I
    have long enough stifled and choked ;
Emblematic and capricious blades I leave you, now you serve me
    not,
I will say what I have to say by itself,
I will sound myself and comrades only, I will never again utter a
    call only their call,
I will raise with it immortal reverberations through the States,
I will give an example to lovers to take permanent shape and
    will through the States,
Through me shall the words be said to make death exhilarating,
Give me your tone therefore O death, that I may accord with it,
Give me yourself, for I see that you belong to me now above all,
    and are folded inseparably together, you love and death are,
Nor will I allow you to balk me any more with what I was calling life,
For now it is convey'd to me that you are the purports essential,
That you hide in these shifting forms of life, for reasons, and that
    they are mainly for you,
That you beyond them come forth to remain, the real reality,
That behind the mask of materials you patiently wait, no matter
    how long,
That you will one day perhaps take control of all,
That you will perhaps dissipate this entire show of appearance,
That may-be you are what it is all for, but it does not last so very
    long,
But you will last very long.

WHOEVER YOU ARE HOLDING ME NOW IN HAND.

WHOEVER you are holding me now in hand,
Without one thing all will be useless,
I give you fair warning before you attempt me further,
I am not what you supposed, but far different.

Who is he that would become my follower?
Who would sign himself a candidate for my affections?

The way is suspicious, the result uncertain, perhaps destructive,
You would have to give up all else, I alone would expect to be
    your sole and exclusive standard,
Your novitiate would even then be long and exhausting,
The whole past theory of your life and all conformity to the lives
    around you would have to be abandon'd,

Therefore release me now before troubling yourself any further, let
    go your hand from my shoulders,
Put me down and depart on your way.

Or else by stealth in some wood for trial,
Or back of a rock in the open air,
(For in any roof'd room of a house I emerge not, nor in com-
    pany,
And in libraries I lie as one dumb, a gawk, or unborn, or dead,)
But just possibly with you on a high hill, first watching lest any
    person for miles around approach unawares,
Or possibly with you sailing at sea, or on the beach of the sea or
    some quiet island,
Here to put your lips upon mine I permit you,
With the comrade's long-dwelling kiss or the new husband's kiss,
For I am the new husband and I am the comrade.

Or if you will, thrusting me beneath your clothing,
Where I may feel the throbs of your heart or rest upon your
    hip,
Carry me when you go forth over land or sea ;
For thus merely touching you is enough, is best,
And thus touching you would I silently sleep and be carried
    eternally.

But these leaves conning you con at peril,
For these leaves and me you will not understand,
They will elude you at first and still more afterward, I will
    certainly elude you,
Even while you should think you had unquestionably caught me,
    behold !
Already you see I have escaped from you.

For it is not for what I have put into it that I have written this
    book,
Nor is it by reading it you will acquire it,
Nor do those know me best who admire me and vauntingly praise
    me,
Nor will the candidates for my love (unless at most a very few)
    prove victorious,
Nor will my poems do good only, they will do just as much evil,
    perhaps more,
For all is useless without that which you may guess at many times
    and not hit, that which I hinted at ;
Therefore release me and depart on your way.

FOR YOU O DEMOCRACY.

COME, I will make the continent indissoluble,
I will make the most splendid race the sun ever shone upon,
I will make divine magnetic lands,
      With the love of comrades,
      With the life-long love of comrades.

I will plant companionship thick as trees along all the rivers of
    America, and along the shores of the great lakes, and all
    over the prairies,
I will make inseparable cities with their arms about each other's
    necks,
      By the love of comrades,
      By the manly love of comrades.

For you these from me, O Democracy, to serve you ma femme!
For you, for you I am trilling these songs.

THESE I SINGING IN SPRING.

THESE I singing in spring collect for lovers,
(For who but I should understand lovers and all their sorrow and
    joy?
And who but I should be the poet of comrades?)
Collecting I traverse the garden the world, but soon I pass the
    gates,
Now along the pond-side, now wading in a little, fearing not the
    wet,
Now by the post-and-rail fences where the old stones thrown there,
    pick'd from the fields, have accumulated,
(Wild-flowers and vines and weeds come up through the stones
    and partly cover them, beyond these I pass,)
Far, far in the forest, or sauntering later in summer, before I think
    where I go,
Solitary, smelling the earthy smell, stopping now and then in the
    silence,
Alone I had thought, yet soon a troop gathers around me,
Some walk by my side and some behind, and some embrace my
    arms or neck,
They the spirits of dear friends dead or alive, thicker they come,
    a great crowd, and I in the middle,
Collecting, dispensing, singing, there I wander with them,
Plucking something for tokens, tossing toward whoever is near me,
Here, lilac, with a branch of pine,

Here, out of my pocket, some moss which I pull'd off a live-oak
    in Florida as it hung trailing down,
Here, some pinks and laurel leaves, and a handful of sage,
And here what I now draw from the water, wading in the pond-
    side,
(O here I last saw him that tenderly loves me, and returns again
    never to separate from me,
And this, O this shall henceforth be the token of comrades, this
    calamus-root shall,
Interchange it youths with each other! let none render it back!)
And twigs of maple and a bunch of wild orange and chestnut,
And stems of currants and plum-blows, and the aromatic cedar,
These I compass'd around by a thick cloud of spirits,
Wandering, point to or touch as I pass, or throw them loosely
    from me,
Indicating to each one what he shall have, giving something to
    each;
But what I drew from the water by the pond-side, that I reserve,
I will give of it, but only to them that love as I myself am capable
    of loving.

NOT HEAVING FROM MY RIBB'D BREAST ONLY.

Not heaving from my ribb'd breast only,
Not in sighs at night in rage dissatisfied with myself,
Not in those long-drawn, ill-supprest sighs,
Not in many an oath and promise broken,
Not in my wilful and savage soul's volition,
Not in the subtle nourishment of the air,
Not in this beating and pounding at my temples and wrists,
Not in the curious systole and diastole within which will one day
    cease,
Not in many a hungry wish told to the skies only,
Not in cries, laughter, defiances, thrown from me when alone far
    in the wilds,
Not in husky pantings through clinch'd teeth,
Not in sounded and resounded words, chattering words, echoes,
    dead words,
Not in the murmurs of my dreams while I sleep,
Nor the other murmurs of these incredible dreams of every day,
Nor in the limbs and senses of my body that take you and dismiss
    you continually — not there,
Not in any or all of them O adhesiveness! O pulse of my life!
Need I that you exist and show yourself any more than in these
    songs.

OF THE TERRIBLE DOUBT OF APPEARANCES.

OF the terrible doubt of appearances,
Of the uncertainty after all, that we may be deluded,
That may-be reliance and hope are but speculations after all,
That may-be identity beyond the grave is a beautiful fable only,
May-be the things I perceive, the animals, plants, men, hills,
    shining and flowing waters,
The skies of day and night, colors, densities, forms, may-be these
    are (as doubtless they are) only apparitions, and the real
    something has yet to be known,
(How often they dart out of themselves as if to confound me and
    mock me !
How often I think neither I know, nor any man knows, aught of
    them,)
May-be seeming to me what they are (as doubtless they indeed
    but seem) as from my present point of view, and might
    prove (as of course they would) nought of what they
    appear, or nought anyhow, from entirely changed points
    of view ;
To me these and the like of these are curiously answer'd by my
    lovers, my dear friends,
When he whom I love travels with me or sits a long while holding
    me by the hand,
When the subtle air, the impalpable, the sense that words and
    reason hold not, surround us and pervade us,
Then I am charged with untold and untellable wisdom, I am
    silent, I require nothing further,
I cannot answer the question of appearances or that of identity
    beyond the grave,
But I walk or sit indifferent, I am satisfied,
He ahold of my hand has completely satisfied me.

THE BASE OF ALL METAPHYSICS.

AND now gentlemen,
A word I give to remain in your memories and minds,
As base and finalè too for all metaphysics.

(So to the students the old professor,
At the close of his crowded course.)

Having studied the new and antique, the Greek and Germanic
    systems,
Kant having studied and stated, Fichte and Schelling and Hegel,

Stated the lore of Plato, and Socrates greater than Plato,
And greater than Socrates sought and stated, Christ divine having
  studied long,
I see reminiscent to-day those Greek and Germanic systems,
See the philosophies all, Christian churches and tenets see,
Yet underneath Socrates clearly see, and underneath Christ the
  divine I see,
The dear love of man for his comrade, the attraction of friend to
  friend,
Of the well-married husband and wife, of children and parents,
Of city for city and land for land.

RECORDERS AGES HENCE.

RECORDERS ages hence,
Come, I will take you down underneath this impassive exterior, I
  will tell you what to say of me,
Publish my name and hang up my picture as that of the tenderest
  lover,
The friend the lover's portrait, of whom his friend his lover was
  fondest,
Who was not proud of his songs, but of the measureless ocean of
  love within him, and freely pour'd it forth,
Who often walk'd lonesome walks thinking of his dear friends, his
  lovers,
Who pensive away from one he lov'd often lay sleepless and dissat-
  isfied at night,
Who knew too well the sick, sick dread lest the one he lov'd
  might secretly be indifferent to him,
Whose happiest days were far away through fields, in woods, on
  hills, he and another wandering hand in hand, they twain
  apart from other men,
Who oft as he saunter'd the streets curv'd with his arm the shoul-
  der of his friend, while the arm of his friend rested upon
  him also.

WHEN I HEARD AT THE CLOSE OF THE DAY.

WHEN I heard at the close of the day how my name had been
  receiv'd with plaudits in the capitol, still it was not a happy
  night for me that follow'd,
And else when I carous'd, or when my plans were accomplish'd,
  still I was not happy,

But the day when I rose at dawn from the bed of perfect health,
    refresh'd, singing, inhaling the ripe breath of autumn,
When I saw the full moon in the west grow pale and disappear in
    the morning light,
When I wander'd alone over the beach, and undressing bathed,
    laughing with the cool waters, and saw the sun rise,
And when I thought how my dear friend my lover was on his way
    coming, O then I was happy,
O then each breath tasted sweeter, and all that day my food
    nourish'd me more, and the beautiful day pass'd well,
And the next came with equal joy, and with the next at evening
    came my friend,
And that night while all was still I heard the waters roll slowly
    continually up the shores,
I heard the hissing rustle of the liquid and sands as directed to
    me whispering to congratulate me,
For the one I love most lay sleeping by me under the same cover
    in the cool night,
In the stillness in the autumn moonbeams his face was inclined
    toward me,
And his arm lay lightly around my breast — and that night I was
    happy.

ARE YOU THE NEW PERSON DRAWN TOWARD ME?

ARE you the new person drawn toward me?
To begin with take warning, I am surely far different from what
    you suppose ;
Do you suppose you will find in me your ideal?
Do you think it so easy to have me become your lover?
Do you think the friendship of me would be unalloy'd satisfaction?
Do you think I am trusty and faithful?
Do you see no further than this façade, this smooth and tolerant
    manner of me?
Do you suppose yourself advancing on real ground toward a real
    heroic man?
Have you no thought O dreamer that it may be all maya, illusion?

ROOTS AND LEAVES THEMSELVES ALONE.

ROOTS and leaves themselves alone are these,
Scents brought to men and women from the wild woods and
    pond-side,

Breast-sorrel and pinks of love, fingers that wind around tighter
than vines,
Gushes from the throats of birds hid in the foliage of trees as the
sun is risen,
Breezes of land and love set from living shores to you on the living
sea, to you O sailors !
Frost-mellow'd berries and Third-month twigs offer'd fresh to
young persons wandering out in the fields when the winter
breaks up,
Love-buds put before you and within you whoever you are,
Buds to be unfolded on the old terms,
If you bring the warmth of the sun to them they will open and
bring form, color, perfume, to you,
If you become the aliment and the wet they will become flowers,
fruits, tall branches and trees.

NOT HEAT FLAMES UP AND CONSUMES.

Not heat flames up and consumes,
Not sea-waves hurry in and out,
Not the air delicious and dry, the air of ripe summer, bears lightly
along white down-balls of myriads of seeds,
Wafted, sailing gracefully, to drop where they may ;
Not these, O none of these more than the flames of me, consum-
ing, burning for his love whom I love,
O none more than I hurrying in and out ;
Does the tide hurry, seeking something, and never give up? O I
the same,
O nor down-balls nor perfumes, nor the high rain-emitting clouds,
are borne through the open air,
Any more than my soul is borne through the open air,
Wafted in all directions O love, for friendship, for you.

TRICKLE DROPS.

Trickle drops ! my blue veins leaving !
O drops of me ! trickle, slow drops,
Candid from me falling, drip, bleeding drops,
From wounds made to free you whence you were prison'd,
From my face, from my forehead and lips,
From my breast, from within where I was conceal'd, press forth
red drops, confession drops,
Stain every page, stain every song I sing, every word I say, bloody
drops,

Let them know your scarlet heat, let them glisten,
Saturate them with yourself all ashamed and wet,
Glow upon all I have written or shall write, bleeding drops,
Let it all be seen in your light, blushing drops.

CITY OF ORGIES.

City of orgies, walks and joys,
City whom that I have lived and sung in your midst will one day
    make you illustrious,
Not the pageants of you, not your shifting tableaus, your specta-
    cles, repay me,
Not the interminable rows of your houses, nor the ships at the
    wharves,
Nor the processions in the streets, nor the bright windows with
    goods in them,
Nor to converse with learn'd persons, or bear my share in the soiree
    or feast ;
Not those, but as I pass O Manhattan, your frequent and swift
    flash of eyes offering me love,
Offering response to my own — these repay me,
Lovers, continual lovers, only repay me.

BEHOLD THIS SWARTHY FACE.

Behold this swarthy face, these gray eyes,
This beard, the white wool unclipt upon my neck,
My brown hands and the silent manner of me without charm ;
Yet comes one a Manhattanese and ever at parting kisses me
    lightly on the lips with robust love,
And I on the crossing of the street or on the ship's deck give a
    kiss in return,
We observe that salute of American comrades land and sea,
We are those two natural and nonchalant persons.

I SAW IN LOUISIANA A LIVE-OAK GROWING.

I saw in Louisiana a live-oak growing,
All alone stood it and the moss hung down from the branches,
Without any companion it grew there uttering joyous leaves of
    dark green,
And its look, rude, unbending, lusty, made me think of myself,
But I wonder'd how it could utter joyous leaves standing alone
    there without its friend near, for I knew I could not,

And I broke off a twig with a certain number of leaves upon it,
    and twined around it a little moss,
And brought it away, and I have placed it in sight in my room,
It is not needed to remind me as of my own dear friends,
(For I believe lately I think of little else than of them,)
Yet it remains to me a curious token, it makes me think of manly
    love ;
For all that, and though the live-oak glistens there in Louisiana
    solitary in a wide flat space,
Uttering joyous leaves all its life without a friend a lover near,
I know very well I could not.

TO A STRANGER.

PASSING stranger ! you do not know how longingly I look upon
    you,
You must be he I was seeking, or she I was seeking, (it comes to
    me as of a dream,)
I have somewhere surely lived a life of joy with you,
All is recall'd as we flit by each other, fluid, affectionate, chaste,
    matured,
You grew up with me, were a boy with me or a girl with me,
I ate with you and slept with you, your body has become not yours
    only nor left my body mine only,
You give me the pleasure of your eyes, face, flesh, as we pass, you
    take of my beard, breast, hands, in return,
I am not to speak to you, I am to think of you when I sit alone
    or wake at night alone,
I am to wait, I do not doubt I am to meet you again,
I am to see to it that I do not lose you.

THIS MOMENT YEARNING AND THOUGHTFUL.

THIS moment yearning and thoughtful sitting alone,
It seems to me there are other men in other lands yearning and
    thoughtful,
It seems to me I can look over and behold them in Germany,
    Italy, France, Spain,
Or far, far away, in China, or in Russia or Japan, talking other
    dialects,
And it seems to me if I could know those men I should become
    attached to them as I do to men in my own lands,
O I know we should be brethren and lovers,
I know I should be happy with them.

I HEAR IT WAS CHARGED AGAINST ME.

I HEAR it was charged against me that I sought to destroy institu-
tions,
But really I am neither for nor against institutions,
(What indeed have I in common with them? or what with the
destruction of them?)
Only I will establish in the Mannahatta and in every city of these
States inland and seaboard
And in the fields and woods, and above every keel little or large
that dents the water,
Without edifices or rules or trustees or any argument,
The institution of the dear love of comrades.

THE PRAIRIE-GRASS DIVIDING.

THE prairie-grass dividing, its special odor breathing,
I demand of it the spiritual corresponding,
Demand the most copious and close companionship of men,
Demand the blades to rise of words, acts, beings,
Those of the open atmosphere, coarse, sunlit, fresh, nutritious,
Those that go their own gait, erect, stepping with freedom and
command, leading not following,
Those with a never-quell'd audacity, those with sweet and lusty
flesh clear of taint,
Those that look carelessly in the faces of Presidents and governors,
as to say *Who are you?*
Those of earth-born passion, simple, never constrain'd, never
obedient,
Those of inland America.

WHEN I PERUSE THE CONQUER'D FAME.

WHEN I peruse the conquer'd fame of heroes and the victories
of mighty generals, I do not envy the generals,
Nor the President in his Presidency, nor the rich in his great
house,
But when I hear of the brotherhood of lovers, how it was with
them,
How together through life, through dangers, odium, unchanging,
long and long,
Through youth and through middle and old age, how unfaltering,
how affectionate and faithful they were,
Then I am pensive — I hastily walk away fill'd with the bitterest
envy.

WE TWO BOYS TOGETHER CLINGING.

WE two boys together clinging,
One the other never leaving,
Up and down the roads going, North and South excursions
making,
Power enjoying, elbows stretching, fingers clutching,
Arm'd and fearless, eating, drinking, sleeping, loving,
No law less than ourselves owning, sailing, soldiering, thieving,
threatening,
Misers, menials, priests alarming, air breathing, water drinking, on
the turf or the sea-beach dancing,
Cities wrenching, ease scorning, statutes mocking, feebleness chas-
ing,
Fulfilling our foray.

A PROMISE TO CALIFORNIA.

A PROMISE to California,
Or inland to the great pastoral Plains, and on to Puget sound and
Oregon ;
Sojourning east a while longer, soon I travel toward you, to remain,
to teach robust American love,
For I know very well that I and robust love belong among you,
inland, and along the Western sea ;
For these States tend inland and toward the Western sea, and I
will also.

HERE THE FRAILEST LEAVES OF ME.

HERE the frailest leaves of me and yet my strongest lasting,
Here I shade and hide my thoughts, I myself do not expose them,
And yet they expose me more than all my other poems.

NO LABOR-SAVING MACHINE.

No labor-saving machine,
Nor discovery have I made,
Nor will I be able to leave behind me any wealthy bequest to
found a hospital or library,
Nor reminiscence of any deed of courage for America,
Nor literary success nor intellect, nor book for the book-shelf,
But a few carols vibrating through the air I leave,
For comrades and lovers.

A GLIMPSE.

A GLIMPSE through an interstice caught,
Of a crowd of workmen and drivers in a bar-room around the
    stove late of a winter night, and I unremark'd seated in a
    corner,
Of a youth who loves me and whom I love, silently approaching
    and seating himself near, that he may hold me by the hand,
A long while amid the noises of coming and going, of drinking
    and oath and smutty jest,
There we two, content, happy in being together, speaking little,
    perhaps not a word.

A LEAF FOR HAND IN HAND.

A LEAF for hand in hand ;
You natural persons old and young !
You on the Mississippi and on all the branches and bayous of the
    Mississippi !
You friendly boatmen and mechanics ! you roughs !
You twain ! and all processions moving along the streets !
I wish to infuse myself among you till I see it common for you to
    walk hand in hand.

EARTH, MY LIKENESS.

EARTH, my likeness,
Though you look so impassive, ample and spheric there,
I now suspect that is not all ;
I now suspect there is something fierce in you eligible to burst forth,
For an athlete is enamour'd of me, and I of him,
But toward him there is something fierce and terrible in me eligi-
    ble to burst forth,
I dare not tell it in words, not even in these songs.

I DREAM'D IN A DREAM.

I DREAM'D in a dream I saw a city invincible to the attacks of the
    whole of the rest of the earth,
I dream'd that was the new city of Friends,
Nothing was greater there than the quality of robust love, it led
    the rest,
It was seen every hour in the actions of the men of that city,
And in all their looks and words.

WHAT THINK YOU I TAKE MY PEN IN HAND?

WHAT think you I take my pen in hand to record?
The battle-ship, perfect-model'd, majestic, that I saw pass the
 offing to-day under full sail?
The splendors of the past day? or the splendor of the night that
 envelops me?
Or the vaunted glory and growth of the great city spread around
 me? — no ;
But merely of two simple men I saw to-day on the pier in the
 midst of the crowd, parting the parting of dear friends,
The one to remain hung on the other's neck and passionately
 kiss'd him,
While the one to depart tightly prest the one to remain in his
 arms.

TO THE EAST AND TO THE WEST.

To the East and to the West,
To the man of the Seaside State and of Pennsylvania,
To the Kanadian of the north, to the Southerner I love,
These with perfect trust to depict you as myself, the germs are in
 all men,
I believe the main purport of these States is to found a superb
 friendship, exaltè, previously unknown,
Because I perceive it waits, and has been always waiting, latent in
 all men.

SOMETIMES WITH ONE I LOVE.

SOMETIMES with one I love I fill myself with rage for fear I effuse
 unreturn'd love,
But now I think there is no unreturn'd love, the pay is certain one
 way or another,
(I loved a certain person ardently and my love was not return'd,
Yet out of that I have written these songs.)

TO A WESTERN BOY.

MANY things to absorb I teach to help you become eleve of mine ;
Yet if blood like mine circle not in your veins,
If you be not silently selected by lovers and do not silently select
 lovers,
Of what use is it that you seek to become eleve of mine?

FAST ANCHOR'D ETERNAL O LOVE!

FAST-ANCHOR'D eternal O love ! O woman I love !
O bride ! O wife ! more resistless than I can tell, the thought of
    you !
Then separate, as disembodied or another born,
Ethereal, the last athletic reality, my consolation,
I ascend, I float in the regions of your love O man,
O sharer of my roving life.

AMONG THE MULTITUDE.

AMONG the men and women the multitude,
I perceive one picking me out by secret and divine signs,
Acknowledging none else, not parent, wife, husband, brother,
    child, any nearer than I am,
Some are baffled, but that one is not — that one knows me.

Ah lover and perfect equal,
I meant that you should discover me so by faint indirections,
And I when I meet you mean to discover you by the like in you.

O YOU WHOM I OFTEN AND SILENTLY COME.

O YOU whom I often and silently come where you are that I may
    be with you,
As I walk by your side or sit near, or remain in the same room
    with you,
Little you know the subtle electric fire that for your sake is play-
    ing within me.

THAT SHADOW MY LIKENESS.

THAT shadow my likeness that goes to and fro seeking a liveli-
    hood, chattering, chaffering,
How often I find myself standing and looking at it where it
    flits,
How often I question and doubt whether that is really me ;
But among my lovers and caroling these songs,
O I never doubt whether that is really me.

FULL OF LIFE NOW.

FULL of life now, compact, visible,
I, forty years old the eighty-third year of the States,

To one a century hence or any number of centuries hence,
To you yet unborn these, seeking you.

When you read these I that was visible am become invisible,
Now it is you, compact, visible, realizing my poems, seeking me,
Fancying how happy you were if I could be with you and become
     your comrade ;
Be it as if I were with you.   (Be not too certain but I am now
     with you.)

SALUT AU MONDE!

1

O TAKE my hand Walt Whitman !
Such gliding wonders ! such sights and sounds !
Such join'd unended links, each hook'd to the next,
Each answering all, each sharing the earth with all.

What widens within you Walt Whitman?
What waves and soils exuding?
What climes? what persons and cities are here?
Who are the infants, some playing, some slumbering?
Who are the girls? who are the married women?
Who are the groups of old men going slowly with their arms about
     each other's necks?
What rivers are these? what forests and fruits are these?
What are the mountains call'd that rise so high in the mists?
What myriads of dwellings are they fill'd with dwellers?

2

Within me latitude widens, longitude lengthens,
Asia, Africa, Europe, are to the east — America is provided for in
     the west,
Banding the bulge of the earth winds the hot equator,
Curiously north and south turn the axis-ends,
Within me is the longest day, the sun wheels in slanting rings, it
     does not set for months,
Stretch'd in due time within me the midnight sun just rises above
     the horizon and sinks again,
Within me zones, seas, cataracts, forests, volcanoes, groups,
Malaysia, Polynesia, and the great West Indian islands.

SONGS OF
MALE INTIMACY
AND LOVE
An Afterword

In the spring of 1859 Walt Whitman meticulously copied
a sequence of twelve poems of male intimacy and love in
a small notebook of white wove paper. Entitled "Live
Oak, with Moss," these poems represent a revolutionary
break with the past and a radical new departure in liter-
ary, sexual, and social history in their moving evocation
and affirmation of the hitherto unnamed and unnam-
able bonds of erotic passion, love, and affection among
and between men. Although this sequence was broken
up and published in revised form as part of the "Cala-
mus" cluster in the 1860–61 edition of *Leaves of Grass*,
like so much in the history of Whitman as man lover
and writer of man-loving poems, the original manu-
script of the "Live Oak, with Moss" poems remained
unknown until 1951, when Fredson Bowers discovered
the numbered sequence among the manuscripts of the
1860 *Leaves of Grass* in the Valentine-Barrett collec-
tion at the University of Virginia. Bowers published the
original numbered version of the "Live Oak, with Moss"
poems in his journal, *Studies in Bibliography*, in 1953.[1]
Oddly, given the importance of this sequence of poems
in the history of literature, sexuality, and men loving
men, "Live Oak, with Moss" has remained largely the
province of scholars and has never been published in an
inexpensive and easily available edition that can be—as
Whitman wanted his poems of manly love and affection
to be—circulated to friends and lovers in the United
States and around the globe.

It was not until 1992 that Alan Helms published what he called the first extensive reading of the "Live Oak, with Moss" poems, in which he concludes: "By shaming Whitman, by isolating, and—most disastrous for a writer—by silencing him, homophobia wins the determining agon of 'Live Oak.'"[2] But Helms's reading of "Live Oak" is in fact not a reading at all: it is based not on the original sequence published by Bowers but on the revised version of these poems published in the 1860 "Calamus" cluster, which Helms returns to their original "Live Oak" order and reprints at the end of his article. Helms's reading has been challenged by Hershel Parker and others who argue that had Helms read the original ("real") "Live Oak, with Moss," he would have realized that these poems are a "gay manifesto."[3]

A close reading of the original version of Whitman's "Live Oak, with Moss" poems, published together with the 1860 and final edition of the "Calamus" poems for the first time in this edition, suggests that since their first publication in 1953, no one has actually *read* "Live Oak, with Moss" because critics have accepted without question Bowers's basic assumption that "the poems appear to be highly *unified* and to make up an *artistically complete story* of *attachment, crisis,* and *renunciation*" (emphasis added). Some forty years later, Helms follows Bowers's assertion: "The love narrative of 'Live Oak' tells a fairly simple story of infatuation, abandonment, and accommodation." Parker makes the same claim: "The sequence traces the course of a man's love for another man, their happiness together, and the aftermath of their relationship, which proves to be only a love affair, not the lifelong union the speaker had hoped for." What "Bowers first recognized," Parker accepts as "a direct, coherent, powerful literary work."[4]

Reading for "a clear story of a love affair with a

man" and what it meant to Whitman "to come out as America's first self-identified 'homosexual,'" Helms finds "a contrary, self-protective impulse in him to hide it or somehow displace it, distance it or sequester it from public view." Parker agrees with Helms's conclusion that in the "Calamus" poems "the prohibition against speaking of homosexual love has triumphed," but he attributes Helms's mistaken reading of the "Live Oak" poems to the fact that he has read the revised and degenerate version of these poems in "Calamus." Had Helms read the "real" rather than the "Calamus" version of these poems, Parker claims, he would have seen that "'Live Oak, with Moss' is an ultimately triumphant account of the poet's accepting his homosexuality and surviving a thwarted love affair."[5]

Helms and Parker participate in a widely shared perception among historians and literary critics that in Whitman's poems of male intimacy and love in "Live Oak, with Moss," in the "Calamus" cluster of the 1860 *Leaves of Grass*, and in the final version of "Calamus" in the 1881 edition of *Leaves of Grass*, Whitman the guilt-ridden homosexual poet was engaged in a persistent and lifelong process of self-censorship, cover-up, and disguise after he had a single isolated love affair or "homosexual crisis" in the late 1850s.[6]

Live Oak, with Moss

By publishing this edition of Whitman's poems of man love, man sex, and desire in their multiple and proliferating versions, I want to invite readers to read these poems and, as Whitman put it in "Song of Myself," "find out for yourself." But I also want to use the occasion of this afterword to think against the traditional and potentially limited critical frames for reading Whitman's man-loving life and the relations among his man-loving poems in "Live Oak, with Moss," the 1860 "Calamus," and the 1881 "Calamus." I want to begin by suggesting that the story Whitman tells in "Live Oak, with Moss" may not be simple, single, or self-coherent; it may be multiple, poetic, and not a simple or single narrative at all; and it may lead not to either "reconstitution" or "accommodation" but to irresolution and proliferation.

I also want to be mindful of the fact that it was only in the late nineteenth and twentieth centuries that the terms "homosexuality," "heterosexuality," and "gay" were invented to describe distinct sexual identities. In reading Whitman's "Live Oak, with Moss" and "Calamus" poems, Bowers uses the word "homosexual" to describe their content, Helms uses the word "homosexual" in quotation marks to describe Whitman's identity, and Parker uses the word "homosexual" to describe Whitman's identity and "gay" to describe the content of his poems.[7] Rather than imposing these later categories on Whitman's revolutionary man-love sequence, I would like to focus on the terms Whitman actually used to name what could—in the popular, legal, and religious language of his time—only be named as onanism, sodomy, bestiality, or the "sin that has no name," often rendered in Latin to prevent its utterance in the American vernacular.[8] What is perhaps most daring and radical about "Live Oak, with Moss" is Whitman's invention of a new language, a poetic language, drawn from a vast discursive field—including the languages of sentimental friendship, romantic love, natural history, the new sciences and pseudosciences of electricity, the body, and phrenology, the working-class vernacular, French *frater-*

nité, and post-1848 revolutionary internationalism—to name and affirm the experience of man sex and love.

Rather than as a coherent story of love, happiness, loss, and reconciliation, "Live Oak, with Moss" might be read as a daring poetic sequence of scenes, or tableaux, in which Whitman gives voice to a full range of fluid and ever-shifting states of body, mind, and feeling in the everyday life of a working-class man who loves men in mid-nineteenth-century America. The poet begins in full-throated rhapsodic voice in "Live Oak" I, identifying his all-consuming sexual desire—"the flames of me, consuming, burning for his love whom I love"—with the regenerative force of nature, of earth, air, fire, and water. Just as "the heat flames up and consumes," "the sea-waves hurry in and out," "the air of the ripe summer" drops "white down-balls of myriads of seeds" in the earth, Whitman affirms, "O I, the same, to seek my life-long lover." While the force of the poet's passion "for his love whom I love" and "my life-long lover" is clear, even in this opening poem it is unclear whether the poet refers to a man, men, a past or current lover or lovers, or some future fantasy lover.

This open, fluid nature of the poet's man love is underscored by the concluding passage in which he associates the poetically moving and erotically suggestive image of "white down-balls of myriads of seeds, wafted, sailing gracefully, to drop where they may" in line three with the ways the poet's "copious soul" in the final lines "is borne through the open air, wafted in all directions, for friendship, for love. —." Although Whitman's use of the languages of spirituality and friendship in the concluding passage might be read as an act of disguising or normalizing this bold expression of man lust and love, the passage might also be read as an act of poetic invention and sexual democracy in which the poet affirms man sex and man love by naming its presence across a field of discourses in which it was previously marginalized, invisible, abjected, or unnamable.

"Live Oak" II is more irresolute. Set in a particular place and time, and seemingly more autobiographical, the poem records a series of facings, time past and time continuous present, in which the poet identifies himself with and against "a live-oak growing" in Louisiana, after which he names his sonnet-like sequence of man-love poems: "And its look, rude, unbending, lusty, made me think of myself; / But I wondered how it could utter joyous leaves, standing alone there without its friend, its lover—For I knew I could not." The poet plucks a twig of the phallic and "lusty" live oak with moss and "place[s] it in sight in my room," but its symbolism is both rejected and claimed: "It is not needed to remind me as of my friends . . . / Yet it remains to me a curious token—it makes me think of manly love." Torn between a romantic ideal of artistic self-sufficiency, uttering "joyous leaves" in solitude, "without a friend, a lover, near," and the pressing urge of "manly love," of which the "unbending, lusty," glistening and phallic live oak is also a "token," poem II adumbrates a crisis of identity and artistic calling that has not been resolved.[9]

Whitman is at his most ecstatic and particular in "Live Oak" III, a dramatic and erotically charged evocation of the happiness of being in love with another man that is among the most beautiful love lyrics in the English language. The poet begins by rejecting the workaday world of carousing, achievement, and fame— even in the capital city—as not "happy," in favor of the pure sensuous joy and anticipation of seeing and being with his lover. The erotic power of the poem rests on withholding its subject, *happiness*, until the very end, first by defining it against the worldly pleasures that are not happiness, then by signifying the purely physical and bodily pleasures of anticipation through the poet's naked and baptismal bath in the sea: "When I wandered alone over the beach, and undressing, bathed, laughing with the waters, and saw the sun rise."

It is only at midpoint in the poem, after this erotic tryst with the sea, that the "coming" of his male lover is revealed as the source of the poet's happiness: "And when I thought how my friend, my lover, was coming, then O I was happy." The poet's thought of his lover "coming" and the sensuous pleasure it arouses—"Each breath tasted sweeter . . . food nourished me more"—continues to build toward the climax that is achieved rhythmically and descriptively by the final release and flow of lines revealing the poet sleeping happily with his lover by the sea:

> I heard the hissing rustle of the liquid and sands, as
>   directed to me, whispering, to congratulate me,—
>   For the friend I love lay sleeping by my side,
> In the stillness his face was inclined towards me,
>   while the moon's clear beams shone,
> And his arm lay lightly over my breast—And that
>   night I was happy.

Far from being shocked by this scene of two men sleeping together as a crime against nature, the rhythmic flow of nature appears to be at one with their erotic union, as the sea congratulates the poet on his love choice—a tribute underscored by the rolling participles that link the "hissing," "whispering" sea to the male lover "sleeping" by the poet's side. But even here, where the poet is at his happiest, the "hissing rustle" of the sea suggests an undercurrent of something that threatens and disturbs.

Although one might read these first three poems as

part of a single story—of love, conflict, and renunciation in favor of personal happiness and love—there is no logical narrative progression through these three poems; indeed, even the titular and ambiguous symbol of the live oak with moss appears once in "Live Oak" II and then disappears in the remainder of the sequence. Like the poems in the 1855 and 1856 editions of *Leaves of Grass*, the poems of "Live Oak, with Moss" move paratactically, by juxtaposition and association rather than by any clear, logical, or linear development. This lack of clear narrative progression is particularly evident in "Live Oak" IV where we find the sublimely happy poet of "Live Oak" III suddenly (and inexplicably) "alone, yearning and pensive," imagining "there are other men" in Germany, France, Spain, China, and Russia, "talking other dialects," who share his love for men and whom the poet could love "as I love men in my own lands."

Reading the sequence as a single love story, Helms interprets the poet's turn away from the actual lover of poem III to "brethren and lovers" throughout the world as part of an overall pattern of "transgression, retreat; transgression, retreat" in "Live Oak" and "Calamus."[10] But what if this sequence is not about monogamous love or a single love story? It is only in the final poem that Whitman uses the singular *man* rather than the plural *men* to describe his love relationships. The poet's fluid movement between the singular "my friend, my lover" and the more indefinite "a friend, a lover" suggests that the poems may be about a spectrum of loves and not a unified love story about love for one man only. Moreover, rather than limiting his love of men to a particular sexual subculture in New York or the United States, Whitman draws on the global language of political internationalism and French notions of *fraternité* to extend his feelings of loneliness and yearning to a global com-

munity of fantasy lovers: "O I think we should be breth-
ren—I think I should be happy with them." [11]

"Live Oak" V might be read as the turning point of
the sequence and potentially in the poet's life, for it is
here that he announces a life-shifting conversion that
leads him to renounce his earlier desire "to strike up
the songs of the New World" in order to pursue his re-
lationship with his lover. "I can be your singer of songs
no longer," the poet writes: "I have found him who loves
me, as I him in perfect love, / With the rest I dispense."
By poem VI, however, the poet appears to have changed
his mind. He will not give up poetry; he will change its
subject. He will turn away from singing the "glory" of
the city and nature to record everyday scenes of man
passion and love, as instanced by "the two men I saw
to-day on the pier, parting the parting of dear friends. /
The one to remain hung on the other's neck and passion-
ately kissed him—while the one to depart tightly prest
the one to remain in his arms." Poetically radical in its in-
sistence on the physical relations and passions of touch-
ing, kissing, and pressing between two male "friends,"
poem VI is also the first to turn, or displace, the gaze of
the poet as man lover outward toward scenes of other
men openly engaged in acts of physical passion in the
public space of the city.

"Live Oak" VII announces a new direction, a direc-
tion anticipated by previous poems in the sequence
but given its fullest and most revolutionary articula-
tion here. Renouncing his former role as epic poet who
"prophesied of The States and led them the way of their
glories," Whitman in effect writes his own epitaph, tell-
ing future bards how to remember him: "Publish my
name and hang up my picture as that of the tender-
est lover, / The friend, the lover's portrait, of whom his
friend, his lover, was fondest." What Whitman both an-

nounces and inscribes is a radically new form of homo-
erotic love lyric, confessional in its urge to delve "under-
neath" the "impassive exterior" of the poet and tell the
secret of his inner man-loving life; romantic and sen-
timental in its evocation of the suffering lover, "lone-
some," "sleepless and dissatisfied at night," and "sick!
sick!," "dreading lest the one he loved" be "indifferent";
pastoral in its flight from the city and convention to the
"woods," "wandering hand in hand, they twain, apart
from other men"; and visionary in imagining and body-
ing forth a new moral order of men loving men: "Who
ever, as he sauntered the streets, curved with his arm the
manly shoulder of his friend—while the curving arm of
his friend rested upon him also."

"Live Oak" VIII is Whitman's most anguished and
candid confession of the "long, sore and heavy-hearted"
experience of romantic abandonment: "Hours discour-
aged, distracted,—For he, the one I cannot content
myself without—soon I saw him content himself with-
out me." What is extraordinary about the poem is the
minute detail and psychic realism with which the poet
records the experience of romantic bereavement and
the fact that these feelings—of betrayal, loneliness,
vulnerability, distraction, shame, and depression—are
being voiced by a man who has been rejected by another
man. It is this fact that intensifies the poet's suffering:

> Sullen and suffering hours—(I am ashamed—but it
>   is useless—I am what I am;)
> Hours of my torment—I wonder if other men ever
>   have the like, out of the like feelings?

As Robert K. Martin observes, "the suffering of the
poet is double, because of his sense of himself as 'differ-
ent' and because of his feeling of abandonment." While
"the feeling is common to rejected lovers," Martin notes,

"it gains particular intensity for the homosexual who wonders if anyone can possibly share his anguish."[12] The poet's assertion, "I am what I am" echoes Shakespeare's "I am that I am" in Sonnet 121, in which he affirms his love for another man against "others' seeing," but for Whitman this secret sorrow harbored in silence becomes its own form of agonizing torment.

The entire second half of the poem is in the interrogative form, taken up with the question of whether "other men ever have the like, out of the like feelings?":

> Is there even one other like me—distracted—his
>   friend, his lover, lost to him?
> [. . .]
> Does he too harbor his friendship silent and endless?
>   Harbor his anguish and passion?
> Does some stray reminder, or the casual mention of
>   a name, bring the fit back upon him, taciturn and
>   deprest?
> Does he see himself reflected in me? In these hours
>   does he see the face of his hours reflected?

The poet's interrogatives function doubly as narration and cure: they give voice to his own bereavement and difference as a means of *coming to terms*, and, as the final lines of the poem suggest, they enact a scene of homoerotic bereavement in which an *other* future rejected lover of men might *come to terms* by seeing "the face of his hours reflected [in me]."[13]

"Live Oak" IX counters the desolation and secret shame of the poet in poem VIII with a dream vision "of a city where all the men were like brothers." Drawing on the religio-spiritual language of America as a "city on the hill" and the international, and specifically French, revolutionary language of democratic brotherhood, the poet imagines a true democracy of the future in which men can live, love, and touch freely and openly in the public space of the city: "O I saw them tenderly love each other—I often saw them, in numbers, walking hand in hand." Presided over by the public expression of "manly love," which "was seen every hour in the actions of the men of that city, and in all their looks and words.—," the poem gives voice to a new ethos of male tenderness and love that indicates the difference between ideal and reality. At the same time, the distance between the wounded and silent man lover of poem VIII and the dream vision of men loving men in public in poem IX marks the possibility of a new direction, a way "out" that the poet is not yet prepared to take.

The last three poems turn away from the dream vision of men loving men publicly in poem IX and return to the theme of secret love. In "Live Oak" X the poet revels in his erotically charged albeit "silent" love for an indeterminate *you*, who may or may not be one of his previous lovers in the sequence: "Little you know the subtle electric fire that for your sake is playing within me.—." The poet's love for "an athlete" in "Live Oak" XI is more fiercely physical, analogous to "something terrible" in the earth, "ready to break forth," but "it" too must remain unspoken: "I dare not tell it in words— not even in these songs" (the paradox here is that the poet's "songs" have already been telling "it in words" though not yet in public). In the concluding poem, Whitman casts himself in the role of teacher to a sexually exclusive group of "silently" man-loving "eleves": "But if through him speed not the blood of friendship, hot and red—If he be not silently selected by lovers, and do not silently select lovers—of what use were it for him to seek to become eleve of mine?" Making use of the French term *élève* to suggest something different from and sexier than the English *student*, Whitman concludes by infusing the conventions of male sentimental friendship with the passions of the body, the blood, and the flow of semen as a form of blood—"hot and red." The sequence ends with a question mark. Whether the poet will pursue this sexually radical and steamy man-loving pedagogy through poetry, lecturing, or some other form remains unclear.

What is clear is that the poet's love for men has become an increasingly fierce and overwhelming force in his life and his work. "Live Oak, with Moss" not only names this love in its ever-shifting, blissful and "terrible" moods and feelings. It also leaves a candid poetic record of several overlapping crises aroused by this love: a crisis of poetic vocation, augured in II and III and reaching a climax in V, in which the poet renounces his role as singer; a crisis of love, adumbrated in poems II and VII, and given full broken-hearted voice in the "taciturn and deprest" lover of VIII; a crisis of identity, evoked in II and voiced in a multiplicity of moods from happy to abject in III, VII, and VIII; a crisis of poetic subject and genre expressed in VI; a crisis of voice leading from the specter of silence in II, V, and VII to its embrace in X, XI, XII; and a crisis of community (or audience) adumbrated in III, IV, V, VII, VIII, and IX, and invoked as a new separatist man-loving direction and pedagogy in the concluding poem.

When Whitman copied these poems into a notebook in 1859, he may have intended them as some kind of *memento mori* of a love affair, possibly with Fred Vaughan, who lived with or near him at the time they were written, or possibly with another man, or even several men over a span of time.[14] They may reach back in time at least as far as a same-sex and possibly cross-race relationship in

New Orleans in 1848, as poem II, with its reference to "a live-oak growing" in Louisiana suggests; and as suggested by Whitman's poem "Once I Pass'd Through a Populous City," which originally evoked a romance with a man in New Orleans—"But now of all that city I remember only the man who wandered with me, there, for love of me"—before Whitman changed the gender from *he* to *she* and added it to the "Enfans d'Adam" (later "Children of Adam") cluster in 1860.[15]

The fact that Whitman neatly copied these poems in a separate notebook suggests that he may not have intended to publish such seemingly autobiographical and confessional poems of male love: that writing this passionate sequence of man-love and man-sex poems became part of a process of coming to terms or preparation for "Death," as suggested by an intriguing note on the verso of an early version of "I Saw in Louisiana a Live-Oak Growing":

> A Cluster of Poems, Sonnets expressing the
>   thoughts, pictures, aspirations &c.
> Fit to be perused during the days of the approach of
>   Death.
> (that I have prepared myself for that purpose.—
> (Remember now—
> Remember then[16]

The poems may have served to remind the poet of the naturalness of the passions of man love that he *now* wants to affirm and celebrate; the erotic pleasure and happiness of being with his lover or lovers that he wants to remember *now*; the name and picture of "the tenderest lover" by which he *now* wants to be remembered; and the dream of a new city of men loving men as the high ideal he *now* wants to achieve. But for what kind of death is Whitman preparing? The social death of loving men in secret; death to the old standards of romantic love; death to the vocation of poet; or a preparation for his own or the nation's death?

Whatever Whitman portended in his preparation for "the approach of Death," the real story here—and it is a triumphant story for all men who have ever loved other men in secret—is not one of silence and repression: it is the story of Whitman's decision to break the silence, to speak publicly in poetry and print by publishing a cluster of poems on men loving men—physically, socially, sexually, spiritually, and naturally, as the very ground of American democracy—in the 1860 *Leaves of Grass*. And this act, in effect, sounded the death knell to an old religious, social, and political order of men loving men in secrecy, silence, and abjection.

Calamus

As a cluster of poems focused on the love between men, "Live Oak, with Moss" played a crucial role in the conception and ordering of the 1860 edition of *Leaves of Grass* and the cluster-organization of all future editions of *Leaves of Grass*. Sometime in the spring or summer of 1859, "Live Oak, with Moss" became the core of this cluster arrangement when Whitman renamed the sequence "Calamus-Leaves" and scattered the notebook poems throughout what eventually became the "Calamus" cluster in the 1860 *Leaves*. Although Parker has argued that Whitman destroyed what was originally a "gay manifesto" when he revised and reconstituted the "Live Oak" poems as part of the "Calamus" cluster, just the opposite may be the case.[17] While "Live Oak" begins with the poet naming his all-consuming love for another man, he ends by advocating a code of secret and silent love, which seems less like a gay manifesto and more like a nineteenth-century version of "don't ask, don't tell." It is only when Whitman bravely decided to publish these poems as part of what he called the "not yet published" standard of passionate erotic love between men in the "Calamus" cluster that they became part of what might be called a gay manifesto. But even here, as a twentieth-century signifier of a distinct sexual identity, the term *gay* might keep us from hearing the deliciously sensuous, erotically fluid, and finally poetic words Whitman actually used in "Live Oak, with Moss" and "Calamus" to give voice to a world of men-loving men.[18]

In the love poems of "Live Oak, with Moss," Whitman flirted with the idea of taking the path pursued by Emily Dickinson around the same time—of retreating from the public sphere of print and publicity. "I can be your singer of songs no longer," he announces in poem V. But unlike that poet, Whitman chose against the path of public renunciation. Rather, and in some sense quite miraculously, he turned in the 1860 edition of *Leaves of Grass* toward an effort to resolve the political crisis of the Union—the paradox of liberty and union, the one and the many—on the level of the body, sex, and homoerotic love.[19]

This effort at personal and political resolution is evident in "Proto-Leaf" (later "Starting from Paumanok"), the long opening poem that would serve as a kind of preface to the 1860 and future editions of *Leaves of Grass*. Rather than allowing himself to be inwardly consumed by the passion of his love for men, Whitman avows to give open expression to the "burning fires" of this passion as the affective and political force that will hold "These States" together:

I will sing the song of companionship,
I will show what alone must compact These,
I believe These are to found their own ideal of manly
    love, indicating it in me;
I will therefore let flame from me the burning fires
    that were threatening to consume me,
I will lift what has too long kept down those
    smouldering fires,
I will give them complete abandonment,
I will write the evangel-poem of comrades and of love,
(For who but I should understand love, with all its
    sorrow and joy?
And who but I should be the poet of comrades?)[20]

Believing, as he wrote in the manuscript of "Proto-Leaf," that "the main purport of America is to found a new ideal of manly friendship, more ardent, more general," Whitman presents the 1860 *Leaves of Grass* as the "New Bible" of the American republic and himself as the evangel-poet and embodiment of a new democratic gospel of "manly love."[21] He envisions the "burning fires" of "manly" passion, or "adhesiveness," as both the affective foundation of political "Union" and a radically democratizing force that will level distinctions between sexes and classes, "vices" and "virtues":

O my comrade!
O you and me at last—and us two only;
O power, liberty, eternity at last!
O to be relieved of distinctions! To make as much of
    vices as virtues!
O to level occupations and the sexes! O to bring all
    to a common ground! O adhesiveness!
O the pensive aching to be together—you know not
    why, and I know not why.
[...]

> O hand in hand—O wholesome pleasure—O one
>   more desirer and lover,
> O haste, firm holding—haste, haste on, with me.[22]

As the preface poem to the 1860 *Leaves*, "Proto-Leaf" reveals a poet newly articulate about his public role as the evangel-poet of those sexual offenders and social outsiders who were—and still are—among the least visible and most oppressed within the putatively liberating but in fact heteronormatizing structures of the liberal state.[23]

The "Calamus" cluster, which originally included forty-five poems, all published for the first time in the 1860 *Leaves of Grass*, represents a radical departure in Whitman's work and in literary, sexual, and social history. Presided over by calamus, a tall and hardy swamp grass also known as sweetflag, with a phallic spadix and hallucinogenic rhizomatic roots, the "Calamus" cluster focuses on the theme of "adhesiveness," which Whitman describes as "intense and loving comradeship, the personal and passionate attachment of man to man." Like the term *amative*, around which he organized the "Enfans d'Adam" cluster, "embodying the amative love of woman—the same as *Live Oak Leaves* do the passion of friendship for man," Whitman borrowed the term *adhesiveness* from the new science of phrenology: *amative* was used to describe physical love between a man and a woman, and *adhesiveness* was used to describe friendship between members of the same sex.[24] As Whitman's use of the oxymoron "the passion of friendship for man" suggests, he reinvented both terms in his effort to create an affirming language of erotic passion and love between men.

In the 1860 *Leaves of Grass*, "Calamus" immediately

follows the 1855 poem "A Boston Ballad, the 78th Year of These States," which critiques the return of a fugitive slave in the town of Boston under the terms of the Fugitive Slave Law and the Compromise of 1850; it thus prepares for the turn away from the law and institutions toward the bonds of manly love as a mean of revitalizing democracy and "The States" in the "Calamus" cluster. The cluster is also preceded by one of the three visual symbols—a globe of the Americas moving into or out of a cloud, the sun setting or rising on the sea, and a butterfly poised on a finger—that appear on the book's cover, back, and spine and throughout the volume as a kind of visual commentary or supplement.[25] In this case, the potentially ambiguous and (now) erotically suggestive geographical figure of a globe of the Americas appears to embody Whitman's notion that America will lead in the generation of new types of manly friendship and love as the globe comes out of (what now seems) a phallic-shaped cloud that points toward the "paths untrodden" of "Calamus."

In the opening poem (later "In Paths Untrodden") Whitman resolves to publish and give voice to the "not yet published" standard of manly love as a form of resistance to the traditional "pleasures, profits, conformities" of public culture and the marketplace. Although the "Calamus" poems are frequently treated as Whitman's most private sequence of poems, they are also his most public and politically engaged. Framed by an appeal to publicity, the "Calamus" sequence seeks to express, enact, and incite new types of "manly attachment" and "athletic love" as the source and ground of a fully realized democratic culture. This emphasis on publicity and public exhibition is evident even in the seemingly more private, separatist, and renunciatory poems of "Live Oak, with Moss": "Publish my name and hang up my picture as that of the tenderest lover," Whitman declared in "Live Oak" VII (now "Calamus" 10).

Although Alan Helms, Hershel Parker, and others have argued that Whitman's decision to publish his "Live Oak" poems as part of the "Calamus" sequence represents a corruption of some originary purity of homosexual feeling and art, their argument has the effect of reprivatizing both homosexuality and art in a way that is contrary to Whitman's brave homoerotic, democratic, and insistently public, political, and spiritual purpose.[26] Drawing on multiple sources—from Plato's notion of the ethical and political force of erotic love and the erotically charged relation between teacher and pupil in the Greek space of the *paideia* to the Christian Gospels, artisan republicanism, the culture of sentiment, and the radical reform energies of the antebellum United States—Whitman tells "the secret" of his "nights and days" not for sensation or sublimation but as an emancipatory act of sexual, political, artistic, and spiritual liberation.

Like the "Live Oak, with Moss" sequence, the "Calamus" cluster does not tell a single story: it works paratactically, by juxtaposition and association, sprouting multiple, sometimes contradictory blossoms and leaves out of the breast of the poet's man-loving heart. Interweaving passionate and confessional poems of male lust and love with political evocations of the future of democracy and the "States," the "Calamus" poems consistently link the personal with the political, creating what Malcolm Cowley has described as a "very strange amalgam" of "cocksucking and democracy."[27] Rather than breaking up the story or stories of Whitman's love for another man or men that he tells in "Live Oak," the "Calamus" cluster elaborates on the man-sex and man-love poems of "Live Oak" and is in many cases more explicit. Whereas in "Live Oak" III, the poet evokes his blissful moment on the beach with his lover in these words, "For the friend I love lay sleeping by my side . . . / And his arm lay lightly over my breast," in "Calamus" 11 (later "When I Heard at the Close of the Day"), Whitman changed these lines to the more sexually unambiguous: "For the *one I love most* lay sleeping by me *under the same cover* in the cool night . . . / And his arm lay lightly *around* my breast" (italics added). Although Whitman reorders the "Live Oak" poems in the "Calamus" cluster, he does this not to cover over the traces of his sexual feeling for men but to redirect it away from silence and secrets toward public expression, proliferation (as in "We're Everywhere!"), and the future of democracy worldwide.

What has most vexed and puzzled critics about the love poems of "Calamus" is their erotic mingling of sex and death. Through the complex symbolism of the "scented herbage of my breast" in "Calamus" 2, Whitman identifies "Death" with his body ("tomb-leaves, body-leaves"), his phallus and semen ("blossoms of my blood"), his erotic desire for men ("O burning and throbbing"), his songs ("my chant of lovers") and their "perennial" bloom "afterwards" ("above death"):

> I am not sure but the high Soul of lovers welcomes death most;
> Indeed, O Death, I think now these leaves mean precisely the same as you mean;
> Grow up taller, sweet leaves, that I may see! Grow up out of my breast!
> Spring away from the concealed heart there!

Here as elsewhere in the "Calamus" poems, death is a kind of ritual sacrifice, or dying to life, associated with the "hungering desires" of man love—"You are often more bitter than I can bear—you burn and sting me." The poet's "chant of lovers" makes him "think of Death" not only because its "leaves" will "be perused best afterwards," but also because "to ascend to the atmosphere of lovers" is in effect to die to ordinary life and to reconnect with eros, the soul of the universe, beyond death: "Death or life I am then indifferent—my Soul declines to prefer."

Crucial to attaining this "high Soul of lovers" is a poetics of visibility, of saying and naming his man sex and man love that lead the poet to spring away from the symbolism of his "emblematic and capricious blades" as a form of concealment:

> Away! I will say what I have to say, by itself,
> I will escape from the sham that was proposed to
>   me,
> I will sound myself and comrades only—I will never
>   again utter a call, only their call.

While Whitman echoes his conversion to man love and the renunciatory voice of "Live Oak," rather than renouncing his poems he will sound his call of manly love as the very condition of the political growth of the United States: "I will raise, with it, immortal reverberations through The States, / I will give an example to lovers, to take permanent shape and will through The States." Speaking in the final lines as a kind of apostle of this new gospel of manly love, Whitman asserts the inextricability of "Love and Death": "Through me shall the words be said to make death exhilarating." Erotic love between men makes "death exhilarating" because it leads to "the real reality," "the high Soul of lovers" beyond "the shifting forms of life," "the mask of materials," and "this entire show of appearance." This death is not an Emersonian or mystical transcendence into a spiritual world apart from the body, as most critics have claimed. Death to "what I was calling life" becomes the basis of a new religion, an ascent "to the atmosphere of lovers" that is achieved not through transcendence but through the body, sex, and homoerotic love.

As such 1860 poems as "Leaves of Grass" 1 (later "As I Ebb'd with the Ocean of Life") and "A Word Out of the Sea" (later "Out of the Cradle Endlessly Rocking") suggest, what distinguishes the 1860 *Leaves of Grass* and the "Calamus" poems in particular is the poet's turn away from what he calls the "beautiful fable" of "identity beyond the grave" and the "apparitions" of the phenomenal world ("Calamus" 7) toward an acceptance of death: "And if the corpse of any one I love, or if my own corpse, be duly rendered to powder, and poured in the sea, I shall be satisfied" ("Calamus" 17); and an affirmation of "he ahold of my hand" ("Calamus" 7) or he who "lay sleeping by me under the same cover in the night" ("Calamus" 11) as "the real something" ("Calamus" 7), "the last athletic reality" ("Calamus" 38), and the "really me" ("Calamus" 40) that will challenge traditional family relations and thus the very ground of Western society and values with the "institution" ("Calamus" 24) and intimacy of male love: "not parent, wife, husband, brother, child, any nearer than I am" ("Calamus" 41).

In "Calamus" the poet's crisis of poetic vocation in "Live Oak" V (now "Calamus" 8) is preceded by "the terrible question of appearances" in "Calamus" 7, which is "answered by my lovers, my dear friends," and followed by a sequence of reorderered "Live Oak" poems that move from the loss of love in "Calamus" 9 (formerly "Live Oak" VIII), the "tenderest lover" of "Calamus" 10 (formerly "Live Oak" VII), and the "happy" man-loving scene on the beach in "Calamus" 11 (formerly

"Live Oak" III). Far from erasing the story of man love in "Live Oak," the "Calamus" cluster retrieves this story not as a lost and secret past but a public and published present of men loving men that, like "the most copious and close companionship of men" in "Calamus" 25, "with sweet and lusty flesh, clear of taint, choice and chary of its love-power" will continue to grow toward the future.

Whitman's poetic reordering of the "Live Oak" poems in the "Calamus" cluster links the crisis of poetic vocation, love, and voice in "Live Oak" with a broader epistemological crisis and a turn not *away* from poetry but *toward* passionate erotic love between men as the "real reality" to which the "Calamus" poems will give voice. The poet's renunciation in "Calamus" 8—"I can be your singer of songs no longer"—is no longer followed by "I have ceased to enjoy them. / I have found him who loves me, as I him in perfect love." These lines are dropped in favor of what turns out to be a less than perfect love: "One who loves me is jealous of me, and withdraws me from all but love." While the lines may be fanciful, they correspond with the difficulties Whitman was having in his relationship with Fred Vaughan, which ended when Whitman went to Boston in the spring of 1860 to prepare for the publication of *Leaves of Grass*. Within the context of the poems that precede and follow it in the "Calamus" cluster, the poet's renunciation—"I am indifferent to my own songs—I will go with him I love"—reads more like a renunciation of the "songs" he was writing *before* he resolved "to tell the secret of my nights and days" in the "paths untrodden" of the "Calamus" poems.

Whereas "Live Oak" XII closes down around a secret and silenced community of men loving men, in "Calamus" this poem (now "Calamus" 42) becomes part of an outsetting and never finally resolved tension between the common reader that Whitman hailed in the 1855 *Leaves of Grass* — "I stop some where waiting for you" — and a more intimate address "only to them that love, as I myself am capable of loving" as the subject, object, and primary audience ("Calamus" 4). At the outset in "Calamus" 3 (later "Whoever You Are Holding Me Now in Hand") the reader is warned, "I am not what you supposed, but far different," and by the end of the poem, those who do not get "that which I hinted at" are invited to "depart." This vexed, ambivalent, and at times combative relationship with the reader continues in "Calamus" 12 — "Do you think it is so easy to have me become your lover?" — and "Calamus" 16, which returns to the confessional voice of "Live Oak" VIII (now "Calamus" 9). "O conscience-struck! O self-convicted!" the poet exclaims in lines that have usually been read as a confession of the guilt and self-loathing the poet feels as a man who loves men. Read within the context of the poet's struggle with a possibly man-loving, derisive, or "puzzled" reader at the outset of this poem, however, the lines appear to be more an attempt to bring the "secretly" man-loving reader to voice by confessing his own guilt and self-derision *not* because he loves men but because he "*secretly* love[s] strangers! (O tenderly, a long time, and *never avows it*)" (italics added).

These poems of more intimate address are interwoven with poems such as "Calamus" 5 ("For You O Democracy") in which the "real" but hitherto secret and unspeakable "reality" of men loving men becomes inextricably linked with the broader sexual, political, and artistic struggle for democracy in America and worldwide. Rather than representing a "lapse" in Whitman's private and radical "homosexual" vision, as Joseph Cady has argued, this extraordinary poem — like the "robust" public kiss as the "salute of American comrades" in "Calamus" 19 (later "Behold This Swarthy Face") and the representation of the "sweet and lusty flesh" and "earth-born passion" of man love as one with the spread of democracy to "inland America" in "Calamus" 25 ("The Prairie-Grass Dividing")—seeks to resolve the paradox of liberty and union and the political crisis of the nation, not through an appeal to law, the Constitution, the courts, or "by arms," but through the erotic force of physical love and intimacy between men. "Affection shall solve every one of the problems of freedom," Whitman writes, representing himself and his poems as the embodiment of "a new friendship" that will "twist and intertwist" the "States" in bonds of comradeship and love:

> The most dauntless and rude shall touch face to face
> lightly,
> The dependence of Liberty shall be lovers,
> The continuance of Equality shall be comrades.
>
> These shall tie and band stronger than hoops of iron.

Whereas the Constitutional founders sought to regulate and control passion, Whitman wants to let it "flame out" as the affective basis of political union and the public culture of democracy. He seeks to fill public space with the "new signs" of male passion and love—with men kissing, holding hands, embracing, and touching "face to face." "I will plant companionship thick as trees along all the rivers of America, and along the shores of the great lakes, and all over the prairies, / I will make inseparable cities, with their arms about each other's necks." Beyond the law, the military, and the abstract and disembodied language of democratic rights, Whitman's "Calamus" poems embody a public culture of men

loving men as a model of the nonstate forms of demo-
cratic affection that will unite America and the world in
ties "stronger than hoops of iron."

As "Calamus" 5 suggests, in the "Calamus" poems
Whitman's political and democratic project becomes in-
separable from his desire to resist both the privatization
of sex and the naturalization of male-female marriage as
the fundamental means of organizing sexuality, social
institutions, and public space:

> It shall be customary in all directions, in the houses
>   and streets, to see manly affection,
> The departing brother or friend shall salute the
>   remaining brother or friend with a kiss.

Whereas in "Live Oak" IX ("I Dream'd in a Dream") the
poet's dream vision of men tenderly loving each other in
the public space of the city is set against the reality of
repression and silence, in the "Calamus" poems Whit-
man turns to the work of bringing this dream city into
being by infusing his poems and democratic culture with
forms of "manly affection" that are neither private nor
always sexual and genital, but public, erotic, and multi-
ple—a practice of everyday life that is visible and perva-
sive. Acts of physical affection and love between men not
only take place in public: they take place *only* in public.

Extending the image of two men passionately kissing,
hugging, and "tightly prest" in each other's arms in "Live
Oak" VI (now "Calamus" 32), Whitman fills his "Cala-
mus" poems and the public space of print with forms of
manly love that include images of himself as "the new
husband" and "comrade," the poet-lover of his readers
and teacher of *élèves*. He is the poet who embodies the
physical passions of adhesiveness, the heaving "sighs at
night," "cries, laughter, defiances," and "many a hun-
gry wish, told to the skies only" as the "pulse of my life"

and the inspiration of "these songs" ("Calamus" 6). He is the "suffering" lover who gives voice to the "anguish and passion" of unreturned love between men ("Calamus" 9), and he is the man who joyously sleeps with his lover outdoors "under the same cover in the cool night" ("Calamus" 11). He is the urban cruiser, who celebrates Manhattan's "frequent and swift flash of eyes offering me love." "Lovers, continual lovers, only repay me" ("Calamus" 18), he writes in lines that subvert notions of the couple and monogamy as the only forms of sexual pleasure and love. He is the "swarthy" comrade who publicly kisses and is kissed by "a Manhattanese"; and he is the lover of strangers and of "other men in other lands . . . in Germany, Italy, France, Spain—Or far, far away, in China, or in Russia or India—talking other dialects" ("Calamus" 19, 23). He is the defiant man lover of "we two boys together clinging," a mobile in-your-face man couple who invade the land, "armed and fearless—eating, drinking, sleeping, loving" ("Calamus" 26); and he is the "unremarked" person who silently holds hands with "a youth who loves me, and whom I love" amid "a crowd of workmen and drivers in a bar-room" ("Calamus" 29). And he is the insecure man lover who fills himself "with rage, for fear I effuse unreturned love," but then realizes: "I could not have perceived the universe, or written one of my poems, if I had not freely given myself to comrades, to love" ("Calamus" 39).

At the conclusion of "Calamus" Whitman returns to and elaborates upon the thematic of secret love that concluded "Live Oak, with Moss." In fact, "Live Oak" X and XII appear in inverted order as "Calamus" 43 and 44, preceded by a poem in which the poet is picked "out by secret and divine signs" by the "Lover and perfect equal!" he has sought "to discover" by "faint indirections" ("Calamus" 41). But this return to the "secret" is a return with a difference. By the conclusion of "Cala-mus," the secret has become open for those who can read the "signs," as the penultimate poem, "Calamus" 44 (later "Here the Frailest Leaves of Me"), suggests: "Here I shade down and hide my thoughts—I do not expose them, / And yet they expose me more than all my other poems." Like Whitman's shifty and ever-shifting relation with the *you* of the reader, the poet's "secret and divine signs" become part of his strategy of intimacy, his creation of an erotic bond of intimacy with future man lovers and readers who share and know his secret— or think they do.[28]

The biggest secret might come, so to speak, not at the end but in the middle of the "Calamus" cluster— in "Calamus" 21, a poem that has puzzled critics, who have noted its lack of any "apparent relationship" to the "Calamus" poems.[29] Through its "faint indirections," this may be one of Whitman's most sexy, joyous, and campy man-love poems if we read the opening lines, "Music always round me, unceasing, unbeginning—yet long untaught I did not hear," as an extended metaphor for the sheer orgiastic pleasure of man sex signified in the poem by the gendered personae engaged not so much in sound-making as in physical feats of sexual prowess: "A tenor, strong, ascending, with power and health"; "A soprano, at intervals, sailing buoyantly over the tops of waves"; "A transparent base" [my favorite], "shudder-ing lusciously, under and through the universe." Then all together: "The triumphant tutti—the funeral wail-ings, with sweet flutes and violins—All these I fill my-self with."

The poet is exhilarated not only by "the volumes of sound"; he is also "moved by the exquisite meanings": "I listen to the different voices winding in and out, striving, contending with fiery vehemence to excel each other in emotion, / I do not think the performers know themselves—But now I think I begin to know them." This sounds like a passionfest of love figured as the pleasure of musical performance. Although it was not until the early twentieth century that to "make beautiful music together" came to signify sexual intercourse, beginning as early as the sixteenth century experiences were likened to music by virtue of the pleasure they gave. Moreover, in 1859, the very year Whitman wrote the poem, the *OED* notes a colloquial American usage of music to refer to pleasure, amusement, fun, and sport: "Jim is a right clever fellow; there is a great deal of music in him." Whitman the lover of men and music, especially opera, may have appropriated the term *music* to express man love and passion, but it is also possible that the term circulated as code for man pleasure and sport in the sexual subculture of mid-nineteenth-century New York. Preceded by Whitman's affirmation of "rude, unbending, and lusty" man love in "Calamus" 20, and followed by his evocation of anonymous sexual exchanges between passing strangers in "Calamus" 22, and surrounded by the "songs" and "chants" of man passion and man love in the "Calamus" cluster, it seems likely that "Calamus" 21 has no "apparent relationship" to the "Calamus" theme because it is not about music or tutti at all but about "the exquisite meanings," voices "in emotion," and "lusciously" sensual and "shuddering" pleasures—or music—of sex with men.

The "Calamus" poems move not toward a separatist poetics and politics of secretly selecting male lovers, as in the concluding poem of "Live Oak," but toward the poet-lover seeking future readers as potential lovers who will carry on the work of creating an openly man-loving future. Whitman insists on his flesh and blood presence and visibility at a particular moment as part of the process of bringing the revolutionary ideals of equality, freedom, and rights into being:

> Full of life, sweet-blooded, compact, visible,
> I, forty years old the Eighty-third Year of The
>   States,
> To one a century hence, or any number of centuries
>   hence,
> To you, yet unborn, these, seeking you.

Like other "Calamus" poems, "Calamus" 45 turns on questions of "visibility" and presence as crucial to the process of "realizing"—of making real by making "compact" and "visible"—the revolutionary promise of a man-loving future: "When you read these, I, that was visible, am become invisible; / Now it is you, compact, visible, realizing my poems, seeking me." Dead and "invisible" to future generations, the poet depends on a future "compact" and visible man-loving reader, or indeterminate *you*, to make and keep "visible" not only the man-loving reality of his poems but the man-loving presence of the poet by seeking him out: "Fancying how happy you *were*, if I *could be* with you, and *become* your lover; / Be it as if I *were* you. Be not too certain but *I am* now with you" (italics added). The participial "fancying" makes it unclear whether the poet is cruising the reader or the reader is cruising the poet. The fluid temporal movement, from past to present to future, from fantasy ("as if") to presence ("I am with you") suggest that through the material signs of his man-loving poems, the poet will "become" the present, future, spectral, or "visible" lover of a man-loving or potentially man-loving reader who will continue to embody and make visible the meaning of the "Calamus" poems. While the "you" with which the "Calamus" sequence ends may be singular or plural, intimate or indeterminate, as elsewhere in the "Calamus" poems and in *Leaves of Grass* more generally, "you" always has a potentially intimate and singular address, not "you" as in everybody but "you" right now "holding me now in hand": "Be not too certain but I am now with you."

Whitman's address to an "unborn" reader of the future in the concluding poem of "Calamus" suggests a transformation in his role as a poet. In the "Calamus" poems as in the 1860 *Leaves of Grass*, Whitman no longer sees himself as the singer of an already existing world; he sees himself as the singer of a new democratic and openly man-loving world he seeks to bring into being through the creation of his poems as "love buds," which will be germinated and brought to fruition by readers "centuries hence." His uncertainty about the future realization of "the new City of Friends" when the poems were published in the fall of 1860, as the nation moved ever closer to the internecine struggle and blood carnage of the Civil War, is suggested by the ambiguous symbolism of the sun rising out of (or falling into) the sea that follows the "Calamus" cluster in the 1860 edition of *Leaves of Grass*.

I Got the Boys

In critical discussions of Whitman's life and work, many have argued that Whitman's "homosexual" love crisis of the late 1850s was sublimated in the figure of the "wound-dresser" during the Civil War, and ultimately silenced and suppressed in the "good gray" politics and poetics of the post–Civil War period.[30] In fact, however, the rhetorics of desire and intimacy among men and the occasions and contexts for their expression in Whitman's work actually proliferated during the Civil War.[31]

Rather than initiating a sublimation or retreat from the homoerotic politics and poetics of the 1860 *Leaves of Grass*, the Civil War reaffirmed and extended Whitman's democratic vision of the love between men as a force for social, political, and ultimately ethical and religious union. The eroticism of male-male physical contact and love pervades Whitman's Civil War poems, including the more public and political context of his famous elegy for Abraham Lincoln, "When Lilacs Last in the Dooryard Bloom'd," where the poet mourns the death of President Lincoln as "lustrous" comrade and lover.[32]

The centrality of physical and public acts of affection between men to Whitman's historical understanding of the Civil War is further suggested by the fact that he incorporated most of "Calamus" 5—"The dependence of Liberty shall be lovers, / The continuance of Equality shall be comrades"—into his effort to come to terms with the blood carnage of the Civil War in his 1865 *Drum-Taps* poem "Over the Carnage Rose Prophetic a Voice."

The Civil War not only affirmed a range of physical and emotional bonds of affection and intimacy between men as the base of a new democratic order; it also gave Whitman a more militant and combative language in which to express his commitment to the ongoing struggle for this order in the post–Civil War period. "I know my words are weapons, full of danger, full of death," the poet declares in "As I Lay with My Head in Your Lap, Camerado," urging his readers to join him in the battle: "Dear camerado! I confess I have urged you onward with me, and still urge you, without the least idea what is our destination, / Or whether we shall be victorious, or utterly quell'd and defeated."[33] Speaking a fluidly double language of homeroticism and democracy, "As I Lay" registers uneasiness as the poet moves away from the true democracy of wartime comradeship toward the potentially oppressive and heteronormatizing structures of peacetime America.

It is ironic that the iconography of the good gray poet came to dominate Whitman's public image and later critical treatments of his life and work during the very years when we have the most specific historical documentation of his intimate relationships with men.[34] "What did I get?" Whitman said of his service in the Washington hospitals during the Civil War. "Well—I got the boys, for one thing: the boys: thousands of them: they were, they are, they will be mine. . . . I got the boys: then I got Leaves of Grass: but for this I would never have had Leaves of Grass—the consummated book (the last confirming word): I got that: the boys, the Leaves: I got them."[35]

In addition to the extensive correspondence that Whitman carried on with the young men he met during the Civil War, Whitman's notebooks and his correspondence with Peter Doyle and Harry Stafford provide a particularly moving record of his emotional and loving attachments to young working-class men. "Dear Boy," Whitman wrote in 1868 to Peter Doyle, a streetcar driver and ex-Confederate soldier whom he met in Washington in 1865: "I think of you very often, dearest comrade, & with more calmness than when I was there—I find it first rate to think of you, Pete, & to know you are there, all right, & that I shall return, & we will be together again. I don't know what I should do if I hadn't you to think of & look forward to." "My darling," he wrote in 1869, "if you are not well when I come back I will get a good room or two in some quiet place. . . . and we will live together, & devote ourselves altogether to the job of curing you." "Good night, my darling son," he wrote in 1870, "here is a kiss for you, dear boy—on the paper here—a good long one— . . . I will imagine you with your arm around my neck saying Good night, Walt—& me—Good night, Pete."[36]

In a notebook entry that appears to refer to the "*enormous* PERTURBATION" of his "FEVERISH, FLUCTUATING" physical and emotional attachment to Peter Doyle, Whitman wrote:

> Depress the adhesive nature
> It is in excess—making life a torment
> All this diseased, feverish disproportionate
>   *adhesiveness*
> Remember Fred Vaughan.[37]

In Whitman criticism, this entry is usually cited as an instance of the poet's attempt to suppress his sexual desire for men in order to transform himself into the safer and more publicly acceptable image of the good gray poet. But at no place in Whitman's notebooks does he suggest that "adhesiveness" is itself "diseased." Rather, like the male purity tracts, what Whitman suggests is that it is "adhesiveness" in excess that makes "life a torment" and must be brought under control. "PURSUE HER NO MORE," Whitman wrote, coyly changing the object of his erotic desire from HIM to HER. But the change once again suggests the fluidity and convertibility of male and female identities and desires in Whitman's work. The poet's perception of his "adhesiveness" as "diseased" and "disproportionate" and "in excess" does not change even if the object of his excessive attachment has been written over.

Although the intimacy between Whitman and Doyle appears to have subsided in the years following Whitman's paralytic stroke in 1873 and his move to Camden, New Jersey, to live with his brother George, by the mid-

1870s he had entered into a passionate love relationship with Harry Stafford, a young man of eighteen to whom Whitman gave a ring as a sign of his deep affection. "My nephew & I when traveling always share the same room together & the same bed," Whitman wrote in 1876 to arrange for a room (and a bed) with Stafford on one of their trips to New York. Their ardent and turbulent relationship lasted several years and had a major impact on Whitman's life. "Dear Hank," Whitman wrote Stafford in 1881, "I realize plainly that *if I had not known you . . . I should not be a living man to-day*—I think & remember deeply these things & they comfort me—*& you, my darling boy, are the central figure of them all*—."[38]

In addition to leaving a written legacy of images of male-male desire that has functioned centrally in the constitution of modern homosexual identities and communities, Whitman also left a visual legacy of portraits, a small cache of "chum" photographs taken with his boyfriends: Peter Doyle in the 1860s, Harry Stafford in the 1870s, Bill Duckett in the 1880s, and Warren (Warrie) Fritzinger in the 1890s.[39] Although these photographs were not "published" until after Whitman's death in 1892 (and they are still little known or remarked upon by Whitman scholars), they were circulated among Whitman's friends and critics during his lifetime and used in the decade after his death both to canonize Whitman as the good gray poet, as in Richard Maurice Bucke's edition of Whitman's letters to Doyle in *Calamus* (1897), and, as in John Addington Symonds's *Walt Whitman: A Study* (1893) and Eduard Bertz's "Walt Whitman: Ein Charakterbild" (1905), to circulate Whitman's visual image as one of the "divine signs" of a newly emerging international homosexual community.

As Ed Folsom argues powerfully in his essay "Whitman's Calamus Photographs," these revisionary portraits stage new identities and new versions of the family, marriage, and social relationships that blur the traditional roles of mother, father, husband, wife, brother, lover, friend.[40] Through their stunning visual enactments of the ways Whitman might be said to speak not so much *for* woman, bride, wife, and mother but *as* woman, bride, wife, and mother, these "family" and "marital" photographs further suggest the mixture and fluidity of gender identity and performance in Whitman's work. In fact, the photographs are all the more striking because they were taken during the last twenty-five years of Whitman's life, the very years when he is said to have sublimated his sexual passion for men in the more conventional roles of the "wound-dresser," the "good gray poet," and the patriotic nationalist. They were also taken at a time when greater public restraints were being placed on the popular and primarily working-class genre of male "chum" photographs.[41]

Revisions

In support of the idea that Whitman retreated from the open expression of manly love in the Civil War years and later, critics have emphasized the changes he made in his "Calamus" poems after he was fired by the Secretary of the Interior, James Harlan, for moral turpitude in 1865. But here again, a close study of the changes that Whitman made in future editions of *Leaves of Grass* reveals no clear pattern of suppressing or even toning down his poems of man lust and love. In fact, Whitman's decision to delete three poems from "Calamus" in the 1867 *Leaves of Grass*—"Long I Thought That Knowledge Alone Would Suffice," "Hours Continuing Long," and "Who Is Now Reading This?"—suggests that he sought not to tone down or suppress his expression of man love but to suppress the more anguished dimensions of his love for men and to blur the distinction between public poet and private lover he set forth in "Long I Thought That Knowledge Alone Would Suffice." After Whitman gave them their final titles in the 1867 *Leaves*, most of the "Calamus" poems remained unchanged in all subsequent editions of *Leaves of Grass*.

If anything, the few changes that Whitman did make in 1867 suggest that the romantic attachments he had formed, with Thomas Sawyer and Lewis K. Brown and other soldiers he met and cared for in the Washington hospitals, as well as with Peter Doyle after the war, had given him a new confidence in avowing his erotic desire for men.[42] To "Sometimes with One I Love," a key poem in affirming the sources of his poetry and his vision in his affection for men, and thus resolving the apparent split between man lover and poet in the 1860 *Leaves*, Whitman added a parenthetical self-revelation: "(I loved a certain person ardently and my love was not return'd, / Yet out of that I have written these songs.)" While these lines might be read in support of the notion that Whitman sublimated his erotic feelings for men during the war years and after, the number of men Whitman "slept with" during these years and the satisfying love relationship he had formed with Doyle at the time the 1867 "Calamus" poems were published bespeak a very active love life with men that was far from being sublimated. As Charley Shively writes of the many romantic attachments and exchanges with men during the Civil War and later that Whitman details and enumerates in his notebooks: "What is most extraordinary in Whitman is the sheer number of men mentioned usually with some identifying fantasy tags."[43]

Whitman envisioned adhesiveness not as sexual only

but as a social relationship, a politics, a new religion, and a metaphysics.[44] It is this metaphysics of male-male love that is the subject of "The Base of All Metaphysics," the only poem that Whitman added to the "Calamus" sequence in the post–Civil War period. Published as the eighth of the "Calamus" poems, right after "Of the Terrible Doubt of Appearances," in the 1871–72 *Leaves of Grass*, "The Base of All Metaphysics" does not sublimate, dilute, or silence Whitman's celebration of erotic love between men as many have argued.[45] Rather the poem reinvents "the new and antique" systems of philosophy—of Plato and Socrates, of Christ and the Christian church, of Kant, Fichte, Schelling, and Hegel—as the base for alternative forms of male passion and love outside the patriarchal, property-based, and reproduction-centered marriage of man and woman. Perhaps influenced by a recent reading of Plato, "whose whole treatment," Whitman wrote, "assumes the illustration of love" by "the passion inspired in one man by another, more particularly a: beautiful youth" ("it is astounding to modern ideas," he added), Whitman represents "the dear love of man for his comrade, the attraction of friend to friend" as the model of an erotic "attraction" that binds man to man, friend to friend, husband to wife, city to city, and land to land across the universe.[46] In "The Base of All Metaphysics," a pervasive and seemingly natural male-female metaphysics of hierarchy and oppression is displaced and denaturalized by an egalitarian and more democratic metaphysics of male-male love.[47]

The only other major change Whitman made in the "Calamus" cluster in the 1871–72 *Leaves* was to move four "Calamus" poems—"Of Him I Love Day and Night," "That Music Always Round Me," "O Living Always, Always Dying," and "What Ship Puzzled at

Sea"—to *Passage to India*, a new volume Whitman published in 1871 as part of his plan to turn away from his "songs of the body and existence" in *Leaves of Grass* toward "thoughts, or radiations from thoughts, on death, immortality, and a free entrance into the spiritual world."[48] Rather than diluting the "Calamus" poems, the removal of these poems has the effect of concentrating and underscoring the more bodily and affective expressions of erotic love in "Calamus"—torrents of passion, the electricity of desire, the flash of eyes on the street, kissing, hugging, touching, walking hand in hand or arm in arm, bodies pressed together on the street or under the same cover at night. Correspondingly, the four poems moved to the "Whispers of Heavenly Death" section of *Passage to India* reaffirm the relation between eros and death, "body leaves" and "tomb leaves," in the "Calamus" poems. It is through the passions of man love that the poet dies to the world and unites with eros as the "soul" of the universe in "Calamus"; and it is through the "love buds" of his poems produced by that erotic— and spiritual—love that the poet perpetuates himself and his love beyond death in *Leaves of Grass*.

Whitman's representation of men loving men as the base of a new social and religio-spiritual order underlies the visionary democracy of *Democratic Vistas* (1871). In this major attempt to come to terms with the problems of democracy in America, Whitman concludes that "intense and loving comradeship, the personal and passionate attachment of man to man," represents "the most substantial hope and safety of the future of these States." "It is to the development, identification, and general prevalence of that fervid comradeship, (the adhesive love, at least rivaling amative love hitherto possessing imaginative literature, if not going beyond it)," Whitman explains in a footnote, "that I look for the counterbalance and offset of our materialistic and vulgar American democracy, and for the spiritualization thereof." Amid what he called the aggressive selfism, vulgar materialism, and widespread corruption of the Gilded Age, Whitman looked not to marriage or to the traditional family but to "the personal and passionate attachment of man to man" as the social and spiritual base and future hope of the American republic. "I say democracy infers such loving comradeship, as its most inevitable twin or counterpart, without which it will be incomplete, in vain, and incapable of perpetuating itself."[49]

Like recent theorists of what Nancy Fraser has called "subaltern counterpublic" spheres, Whitman imagines a collective popular will that exists apart from the authority of the state.[50] The state is the legal structure of democracy; the people are its base and future. Beyond a first stage of rights and a second stage of material progress and wealth, Whitman theorizes a future public culture of democracy that will be achieved not by law, by government, or by the market, but by the erotic force of adhesive or manly love, which will bind the nation in a living union. This is what Whitman means when in the preface to the 1876 centennial edition of *Leaves of Grass* he writes that

the special meaning of the "Calamus" cluster of "Leaves of Grass," (and more or less running through the book, and cropping out in "Drum-Taps,") mainly resides in its political significance. In my opinion, it is by a fervent, accepted development of comradeship, the beautiful and sane affection of man for man, latent in all the young fellows, north and south, east and west—it is by this, I say, and by what goes directly and indirectly along with it that the United

> States of the future, (I cannot too often repeat,) are
> to be most effectually welded together, intercalated,
> and anneal'd into a living union."[51]

In the very midst of his announcement of his turn
toward spirituality and death in his 1876 preface, Whit-
man reaffirms the notion of adhesiveness as a "terrible,
irrepressible yearning" shared by "all" young men in the
United States—a radical assertion that all men are in
effect "latent" lovers of men; and it is not until this "fer-
vent" love between men is developed and accepted that
democracy in America will achieve its fullest spiritual
and religious realization. Rather than retreating from
the man-love poems of "Calamus," Whitman insists on
their significance to the political future of the United
States, a meaning not limited to a single cluster or a
single moment in 1860, but one that runs "more or less"
throughout *Leaves of Grass*.

The changes in the final 1881 "Calamus" are not so
much to the poems themselves, but to the arrangement
of the poems, especially the new priority of place given
to the "Calamus" cluster in the structure of *Leaves of
Grass*. While these changes in arrangement may seem
insignificant, Whitman's paratactic style—his juxta-
position of words, images, lines, and units without any
express connection—is as characteristic of individual
poems as it is of individual clusters, and the overall
ordering of *Leaves of Grass*. By rearranging the order of
poems and changing the juxtapositions, Whitman em-
phasizes new connections within and among the "Cala-
mus" poems. By placing "Earth, My Likeness" (origi-
nally "Calamus" 36) just before "I Dream'd in a Dream"
(originally "Calamus" 34), Whitman not only connects
the poet's "fierce and terrible" but natural feelings for an
athlete with a "new city" and the dream of a democratic

future in which those feelings can "burst forth." Further, by preceding the dream of men loving men openly in the new city of the future with the temporal "now" of man love about "to burst forth," Whitman suggests an inevitable erotic force and movement toward that future of man love that is always already available and "eligible" at any moment to become "now." He underscores this temporal "now" by following "I Dream'd" with "What Think You I Take My Pen in Hand?" (originally "Calamus" 32), in which he records an actual scene in "the great city spread around me" of passionate love between "two simple men I saw to-day on the pier in the midst of the crowd."

Here as elsewhere in the 1881 *Leaves of Grass*, many new erotic connections, energies, temporalities, and movements are released by the final ordering of poems and clusters. Given the pervasive critical emphasis on the sexual retreat of late Whitman, perhaps the most radical and striking reordering of *Leaves* is the new priority of place and new interpretive possibilities he gave to "Children of Adam" and "Calamus" by having both clusters directly follow "Song of Myself."

Whereas in the 1860 *Leaves* "Calamus" was located on the margins in the final quarter of the volume, separated from "Children of Adam," which preceded it by some fifty pages, by 1881 "Calamus" had been moved front and center, following directly from "Children of Adam" for the first time. In traditional accounts of Whitman's poetic development, "Children of Adam" has been treated as an afterthought—a sequence of poems that Whitman added to the 1860 edition of *Leaves of Grass* in order to provide a legitimizing heterosexual context for the more radical, personal love poems to men in the "Calamus" sequence.[52] But as expressions of sex and the body, the "Children of Adam" poems may in fact be the sexually radical sequence that Emerson and the censors who banned *Leaves of Grass* in Boston in 1882 always believed it to be. A notebook entry suggests that Whitman initially conceived of "Children of Adam" as a companion piece to his "Live Oak, with Moss" poems: "A string of Poems (short, etc.), embodying the amative love of woman—the same as *Live Oak Leaves* do the passion of friendship for man."[53] Whatever Whitman's initial intentions, the "Children of Adam" poems do not read as a neatly "amative" or heterosexual counterpart to his poems of passion for men in the "Live Oak" sequence. (And here it is perhaps important to remember that the term *heterosexual* actually came later than the term *homosexual* in the construction of modern sexuality.) Though the "Children of Adam" poem "A Woman Waits for Me" (initially published in 1856 as "Poem of Procreation") consistently provoked nineteenth-century censorship for its representation of an athletic, sexually charged, and desiring female body, the poem is in fact atypical in its emphasis on the amative, and ultimately procreative and eugenically productive, love between men and women.

"Singing the phallus" and the "bedfellow's song," many of the "Children of Adam" poems are not about women or procreation or progeny at all but about amativeness as a burning, aching, "resistless," emphatically physical "yearning" for young men ("From Pent-Up Aching Rivers"). By having "Children of Adam" directly follow "Song of Myself" in the 1881 *Leaves of Grass*, Whitman underscores its relation to the "voices of sexes and lusts, voices veil'd and I remove the veil" in "Song of Myself." These "forbidden" voices of man sex and man love are particularly evident in the scene of lovemaking between men in section 5 ("Isn't this cocksucking plain and simple?" Charley Shively has asked)[54]; the erotic cross-dressed tryst in the water not with one or two, but "twenty-eight young men [who] bathe by the shore" in section 11; and the scene of man sex or mutual masturbation as a site of ecstasy, vision, and poetic utterance in section 28 ("My flesh and blood playing out lightning to strike what is hardly different from myself"); not to mention the "gigantic beauty of a stallion, fresh and responsive to my caresses . . . / His nostrils dilate as my heels embrace him, / His well-built limbs tremble with pleasure" as code for the "forbidden" pleasure of anal sex between men in section 32.[55]

By moving directly from "Song of Myself" to "Children of Adam" to "Calamus," Whitman links the erotic scenes of man love and passion in "Song of Myself" with the bodily sex and desire of amative love in "Children" and the man love, passions, and yearnings of adhesiveness in "Calamus." Whereas in the "Calamus" poems physical love between or among men is represented in images of men passionately desiring, touching, hugging, pressing, kissing, and sleeping together, in the "Children of Adam" poems Whitman, in the figure of a "lusty," "tremulous," and insistently "phallic" Adam, names and bathes his songs in an active, orgiastic, and fleshy sexuality among men. "Give me now libidinous joys only," the poet declares in "Native Moments," evoking scenes of nonreproductive sexual play and pleasure among men that recall similar scenes of "intemperance" in Whitman's novel *Franklin Evans*:

> I am for those who believe in loose delights, I share
>   the midnight orgies of young men,
> I dance with the dancers and drink with the
>   drinkers,
> The echoes ring with our indecent calls, I pick out
>   some low person for my dearest friend,

He shall be lawless, rude, illiterate, he shall be one
    condemn'd by others for deeds done,
I will play a part no longer, why should I exile myself
    from my companions?[56]

Even "A Woman Waits for Me" is as much a celebration
of a deliciously phallic male sexuality as it is a celebra-
tion of sexual love between men and women. Associat-
ing the woman in the poem with traditionally masculine
activities, the language of the poem slips ambiguously
between celebrations of same-sex and opposite-sex love.
Moreover, in the 1881 edition of *Leaves of Grass*, Whit-
man actually edited out several of the more explicit
references to love between man and woman in the 1860
"Enfans d'Adam" cluster while retaining the emphasis
on an insistently phallic and physical male sexuality.
Thus, Whitman's deletion of the phrase "I take for my
love some prostitute" in the 1860 "Native Moments"
ends up underscoring the "libidinous joys" and "loose
delights" of an explicitly same-sex sexuality among and
between men.[57]

Rather than presenting "Children of Adam" and
"Calamus" as a neatly heterosexual and homosexual
pairing, in the 1881 *Leaves* these clusters bleed into each
other, blurring the distinctions and boundaries between
amative and adhesive love. The final arrangement fur-
ther accentuates the fluid relationship between the
"lusty, phallic" and ultimately nonreproductive and
nonmonogamous sexual play and pleasure among men
in the "Children of Adam" poems and the less insistently
phallic but nonetheless explicitly physical lover and
democrat of the "Calamus" poems. "Touch me, touch
the palm of your hand to my body as I pass, / Be not
afraid of my body," says the naked Adamic speaker in
the final poem of the "Children of Adam" sequence, as

he passes and steps quite imperceptibly into the "paths untrodden" and more emphatically (but not exclusively) male contexts of the "Calamus" poems.[58]

Against popular nineteenth-century associations of masturbation and excessive adhesiveness among men with solitude, impotence, and emasculation, Whitman extended and hybridized the social meanings of *adhesiveness*—the phrenological term for friendship—to signify intense and passionate love between men as a virile and politically productive force for urban, national, and international community. He also extended the meanings of *amativeness*—the phrenological term for procreative love between men and women—to include physical and procreative love among men. Implicit in the sexual and social vision of "Children of Adam" is a New World garden and a new American republic ordered not by the traditional marital, procreative, familial, and monogamous bonds between men and women but by the sexually and socially productive and nonmonogamous bonds among men. While "Children of Adam" appears to refer to *all* the children produced (presumably) by Adam and Eve, as the exclusive emphasis on Adam in the title suggests, these children are also the male children produced and "prepared for" by the "act divine" and "stalwart loins" of a phallic and virile Adam, whose sexual union with men bears the creative and procreative seeds of poetry, American polity, and the future of democracy worldwide.

In his important article "'Here Is Adhesiveness': From Friendship to Homosexuality," Michael Lynch argues that when, in the 1856 edition of *Leaves of Grass* Whitman wrote, "Here is adhesiveness—it is not previously fashioned—it is apropos," in reference to exclusively same-sex relationships among men, his words marked a major shift toward a definition of the homosexual and the heterosexual as distinct types. "Whitman's restriction of Adhesiveness to male-male relationships opened the way for an understanding of same-sex expression of a sexual instinct that was polar to an opposite-sex expression of it." Rather than representing the emergence of what Lynch calls "a distinct 'homosexual identity' and 'homosexual role,'"[59] I would argue that Whitman's "Calamus" and "Children of Adam" poems imply just the opposite. By conceptualizing and articulating his love for men in the language of democratic comradeship and by celebrating physical pleasure among men in the context of male and female amativeness and procreation, Whitman suggests the extent to which the bounds between private and public, male and female, heterosexual and homosexual are still indistinct, permeable, and fluid in his work.

Whoever You Are Holding Me Now in Hand

Ironically, for all the sex radicalism of Whitman's "Calamus" poems, it was the sexually charged women of "Children of Adam," especially "A Woman Waits for Me," the poet's "lusty" solicitation of a female prostitute in "To a Common Prostitute," and the sheer "amorous" pleasure of the one-night stand (among eagles, no less) in "The Dalliance of the Eagles" that got Whitman into trouble: first with Emerson, who begged Whitman to drop the "Enfans d'Adam" poems in the 1860 *Leaves* during their famous walk on the Boston Common; later with the secretary of the interior, who fired Whitman for "moral turpitude" in 1865; and finally with the Boston district attorney, Oliver Stevens, who on March 1, 1882, initiated proceedings to suppress the 1881 edition of *Leaves of Grass* as "obscene literature."[60] Before the term *homo-*

sexuality was first used by the German-Hungarian jour-
nalist Karl Maria Kertbeny in 1892, male-female and
especially female sexuality were under more scrutiny
and surveillance than the still unpoliced range of affec-
tions and sexualities among and between men.[61]

By the end of the century, however, Whitman was
contacted, visited, and after his death celebrated as a
prophet of new forms of sexual tolerance and acceptance
by many sex radicals in Europe, including Edward Car-
penter, Oscar Wilde, and John Addington Symonds in
England, André Gide in France, and Eduard Bertz and
Thomas Mann in Germany.[62] John Addington Symonds,
who first wrote to Whitman in 1871, was the most persis-
tent in urging Whitman to name the sexual love between
men at the heart of the "Calamus" poems.[63] Their most
famous exchange took place in 1890 when, after years
of indirection, Symonds asked Whitman outright if his
"conception of Comradeship" included the possibility of
"semi-sexual emotions & actions" between men. Rather
than telling "the secret of my nights and days," as the
poet promised at the outset of his "Calamus" poems,
Whitman disavowed Symonds's "morbid inferences"
as "undream'd," "unreck'd," and "damnable" and cau-
tioned him about the necessity of construing "all parts
& pages" of *Leaves of Grass* "by their own ensemble,
spirit & atmosphere."[64] Although Whitman's response
is coy, it is also symptomatic of the difference between
the urban, democratic, and working-class sexual sub-
culture in which Whitman circulated and the cosmo-
politan, aristocratic, and upper-class homosocial world
of Symonds. Whitman and Symonds were speaking
two different though not entirely separable languages.
Whereas Havelock Ellis and Symonds were central to
the process of medicalizing and singling out the homo-
sexual as abnormal and pathological, Whitman was

talking about physical and emotional love between men as the basis for a new social and religious order.[65] Given his representation of male sexual love as the source of spiritual and poetic vision and the ground for a new democratic social order, and given Ellis's and Symonds's medicalization of physical love between men as "sexual inversion" and "abnormal instinct," it makes sense that Whitman would disavow Symonds's attempt to medicalize and sexually categorize the "Calamus" poems as "morbid inferences" contrary to the "ensemble, spirit & atmosphere" of *Leaves of Grass*.[66]

Whitman's famous assertion, in this same letter to Symonds, that he had fathered six children is, to say the least, disingenuous. But it is not wholly at odds with the amative, reproductive, and familial languages and contexts in which he expressed loving relationships among and between men. In fact, given the languages of paternal, maternal, and familial affection in which Whitman carried on his relationships and correspondence with Fred Vaughan, Peter Doyle, Harry Stafford, and some of the soldiers he met during the war, including Tom Sawyer and Lewis Brown, one might argue that Whitman was thinking of some of the "illegitimate sons" he adopted, fathered, and mothered over the course of his life.

In the final decades of his life, Whitman was surrounded and protected by a group of "disciples," most notably Richard Maurice Bucke and Horace Traubel, who were dedicated to keeping Whitman's manly love pure, spiritual, and cosmic rather than fleshy, sensual, and homoerotic.[67] Whereas Whitman's man-loving life and poems became central to the emergence and definition of a modern homosexual community in Europe, where the question of Whitman's sexual love of men and alternative readings of his work became the site at once of homosexual self-definition and international scandal in countries such as England, France, and Germany, in the United States Whitman's sexual love of men went underground to become what Cowley called "The Secret."[68] This "secret" split American criticism into two warring parties: those who celebrated Whitman as the prophet of democracy and a new religion of humanity, from Richard Maurice Bucke to James E. Miller Jr.; and those who dismissed his man-loving poems as pathological, narcissistic, and immature—from the "disgust" with "the language of his evangel poems" expressed by a writer in the *Gentleman's Magazine* in 1875 to F. O. Matthiessen and Edwin Haviland Miller.[69] As I have argued elsewhere, this split still dominates the public memory of Whitman's life and work, from debates about naming the Walt Whitman Bridge in 1955–56, to the fact that no government-sponsored events were held in Washington, D.C., to commemorate the centennial of Whitman's death in 1992, to the virtual erasure of Walt Whitman's man-loving life in the exhibit mounted at the Whitman Birthplace Museum in Huntington, Long Island, in 1997, to Laura Bush's abrupt cancellation of "Poetry and the American Voice" in 2003, when she realized that a White House gathering to discuss the poetry of Walt Whitman, Emily Dickinson, and Langston Hughes might turn political.

In 1966 Gavin Arthur, the grandson and namesake of Chester Arthur, the former president of the United States, inaugurated a countertradition that linked Whitman's love seeds with real rather than metaphoric, sublimated, or imaginary sex between men. Arthur's memoir, *The Circle of Sex*, recounts a 1923 visit to Edward Carpenter's cottage in England, where the seventy-eight-year-old Carpenter stroked and caressed and made love to the young man in the same manner that Whitman made love to Carpenter when he visited the poet for several weeks in 1877 and 1884. Whereas in *The Circle of Sex* Arthur describes a form of *karezza*—or body stroking—that led not to a spilling of seed but to "a far more intense orgasm of the whole nervous system in which oneself, as a unit, reunites with the Whole," [70] in 1967 Arthur gave Allen Ginsberg a more erotically detailed account of sleeping with Carpenter, which was later published in *Gay Sunshine* in 1978. "The old man at my side was stroking my body with the most expert touch," Arthur recalled:

> I had of course a throbbing erection but he ignored it for a long time. Very gradually, however, he got nearer and nearer, first with his hand and later with his tongue which was now flickering all over me like summer lightning. I stroked whatever part of him came within reach of my hand but I felt instinctively that this was a one-sided affair, he being so old and I so young, and that he enjoyed petting me as much as I delighted in being petted. . . . At last his hand was moving between my legs and his tongue was in my bellybutton. And then when he was tickling my fundament just behind the balls and I could not hold it longer, his mouth closed just over the head of my penis and I could feel my young vitality flowing into his old age. [71]

Arthur's tender and loving memory of Carpenter making love to him as Whitman made love to Carpenter literalizes Whitman's "Poets to Come," his love buds as seeds wafted to generations hence, in a real scene of men making love. In the history of Whitman's reception, this erotic remembrance has become part of what Allen Ginsberg has called a "line of transmission"—from Whitman to Carpenter to Arthur to Neal Cassady to Ginsberg himself[72]—that embodies, as Whitman's "Calamus" poems embodied, his vision of erotic love between men as the source of poetic utterance, democratic union, and spiritual communion; or, as Gavin Arthur put it, a "laying on of hands," "in which oneself, as a unit, reunites with the Whole."

NOTES

1. Fredson Bowers, "Whitman's Manuscripts of the Original 'Calamus' Poems," *Studies in Bibliography* 6 (1953): 257–65; see also *Whitman's Manuscripts: Leaves of Grass (1860), A Parallel Text*, ed. Fredson Bowers (Chicago: University of Chicago Press, 1955).

2. Alan Helms, "Whitman's 'Live Oak with Moss,'" in *The Continuing Presence of Walt Whitman: The Life after the Life*, ed. Robert K. Martin (Iowa City: University of Iowa Press, 1992), 190.

3. Hershel Parker, "The Real 'Live Oak, with Moss': Straight Talk about Whitman's 'Gay Manifesto,'" *Nineteenth-Century Literature* 51 (September 1996): 145–60.

4. Bowers, "Whitman's Manuscripts," 264; Helms, "Whitman's," 87; Parker, "The Real," 146, 148; see also Steven Olsen-Smith, "'Live Oak, with Moss,' 'Calamus,' and 'Children of Adam,'" in *A Companion to Walt Whitman*, ed. Donald D. Kummings (Malden, MA: Blackwell, 2006), 508.

5. Helms, "Whitman's," 186, 190, 191; Parker, "The Real," 157.

6. For a refreshing rejoinder to this line of criticism, see Mark Doty: In "the realm of the impermissible," he writes, "Whitman astonishes over and over with his forthrightness. From 1855 till the final edition of *Leaves* in 1892, three years before the trial of Oscar Wilde, he persisted in importing the unnamed into the public world of the sayable"; in "Form, Eros, and the Unspeakable: Whitman's Stanzas," *Virginia Quarterly Review* 81 (Spring 2005), 72.

7. Against this tendency to locate "a core 'gay' identity" in Whitman's "Calamus" poems, see Jay Grossman, who argues that the "Calamus" poems "offer over and again a multiplicity of speaking positions without pinning down a single stable location"; in "'The Evangel-Poem of Comrades and of Love': Revis-

ing Whitman's Republicanism," *American Transcendental Quarterly* 4 (September 1990): 209. See also Betsy Erkkila, "Whitman and the Homosexual Republic," in *Walt Whitman: The Centennial Essays*, ed. Ed Folsom (Iowa City: University of Iowa Press, 1994), 153–71; and John Champagne, who argues that the contemporary commodification of Whitman as a gay or homosexual poet tends to simplify the history of sexuality and to blunt the power of Whitman's poetry to queer normative understandings of sex and gender identity and their relationship to politics; in "Walt Whitman, Our Great Gay Poet?" *Journal of Homosexuality* 55 (2008): 648–64.

8. Thus, for example, in his 1855 review of the first edition of *Leaves of Grass*, Rufus Griswold seeks to expose Whitman as a "monster" of "gross obscenity" without offending "ears polite" by concluding his review with the Latin phrase: "*Peccatum illud horribile, inter Christianos non nominandum*" ("a sin so vile that it is not spoken by Christians"); reprinted in *Walt Whitman: The Contemporary Reviews*, ed. Kenneth M. Price (New York: Cambridge University Press, 1996), 27.

9. Insofar as "Live Oak, with Moss" registers this dual reference to artistic utterance and manly love, it might explain why Whitman turned toward the more insistently phallic spadix and proliferating leaves of "Calamus" in the 1860 *Leaves of Grass*. For a more extensive discussion of the tension and anxiety in this poem, see Kerry C. Larson, *Whitman's Drama of Consensus* (Chicago: University of Chicago Press, 1988), 176–79; and Michael Moon, *Disseminating Whitman: Revision and Corporeality in* Leaves of Grass (Cambridge, MA: Harvard University Press, 1991), 163–66.

10. Helms, "Whitman's," 189.

11. Not coincidentally, later some of "them," like Edward Carpenter in England, André Gide in France, and Thomas Mann in Germany, thought they could be happy with Whitman too. See Eve Kosofsky Sedgwick, "Toward the Twentieth Century: English Readers of Whitman," in *Between Men: English Literature and Male Homosocial Desire* (New York: Columbia University Press, 1985), 201–17; Betsy Erkkila, *Walt Whitman among the French: Poet and Myth* (Princeton: Princeton University Press, 1980); Walter Grünzweig, *Constructing the German Walt Whitman* (Iowa City: University of Iowa Press, 1995).

12. Robert K. Martin, *The Homosexual Tradition in American Poetry* (Austin: University of Texas Press, 1979), 68, 69. See also

Helms, who writes of this passage: "Whitman's sense of shame and isolation will be painfully familiar to most lesbians and gay men as part of the process of coming out. 'Is there even one other like me?' is a question that gay men and lesbians have asked themselves by the millions" ("Whitman's," 190).

13. In "'Hours Continuing Long' as Whitman's Rewriting of Shakespeare's Sonnet 29," *Walt Whitman Quarterly Review* 26 (Winter 2009), Nils Clausson argues that in this poem Whitman rewrites Shakespeare's address to a beautiful youth in Sonnet 29 ("When in disgrace with fortune and men's eyes"), giving the personal and psychological focus of the traditional love sonnet a social and political significance: "This poem is not only an expression of Whitman's personal situation, the traditional subject matter of a love sonnet, but also a political meditation on the absence of a community of similar men who experience the same feelings as Whitman does" (139).

14. Charley Shively was the first to identify Fred Vaughan as the inspiration of the "Calamus" poems, in *Calamus Lovers: Walt Whitman's Working-Class Camerados*, ed. Charley Shively (San Francisco: Gay Sunshine Press, 1987), 114, 36–50. See also Gary Schmidgall, *Walt Whitman: A Gay Life* (New York: Dutton, 1997); and Jonathan Ned Katz, *Love Stories: Sex between Men before Homosexuality* (Chicago: University of Chicago Press, 2001).

15. While this might appear to support the notion that Whitman was trying to cover over his relations with men, he was way short on procreative experience and what he called after phrenology "amative" love. Whitman's decision to change the pronouns may have been merely strategic: he needed more "amative" poems to balance the "Enfans d'Adam" with the "Calamus" cluster, for which he had many more poems; see Robert J. Scholnick, "The Texts and Contexts of 'Calamus': Did Whitman Censor Himself in 1860?" *Walt Whitman Quarterly Review* 21 (Winter 2004): 126.

16. Bowers, *Whitman's Manuscripts*, lxvi–lxvii, n8.

17. Parker, "The Real."

18. In *Calamus Lovers*, Shively notes that by the 1860s Whitman and his boy lovers were already using the term *gay* with man-loving connotations (23–24). But in the examples he gives, the term is still being used as an adjective. It was not until the twentieth century that *gay* was used to signify a distinct sexual identity.

19. "The insistent keynote of these poems," Jay Grossman argues, "is not what critics usually emphasize—a marginalized and half–silenced attempt to 'sing' a defeated homosexual self. Rather, the poems militate against a strict privatization, insisting upon the public gestures of confession and, significantly, action" ("The Evangel-Poem," 214). See also Betsy Erkkila, "Public Love: Whitman and Political Theory," in *Whitman East and West: New Contexts for Reading Walt Whitman*, ed. Ed Folsom (Iowa City: University of Iowa Press, 2002), 115–44; and David Groff, who writes: "Men who love men have long seen themselves shunted off to the side roads of their cultural story. Whitman places those men at the center of his epic work"; in *Whitman's Men: Walt Whitman's Calamus Poems Celebrated by Contemporary Photographers* (New York: Universe Publishing, 1996), 8.

20. Walt Whitman, *Leaves of Grass, 1860: The 150th Anniversary Facsimile Edition*, ed. Jason Stacy (Iowa City: University of Iowa Press, 2010), 10–11.

21. Bowers, *Whitman's Manuscripts*, 12.

22. *Leaves of Grass 1860*, 22.

23. Not coincidentally, John Stuart Mill's important essay *On Liberty* was published in 1859. Although Whitman was an admirer of Mill (he cites him at the beginning of his revised edition of *Democratic Vistas*), as Jürgen Habermas observes, Mill's essay marks a growing distinction between liberal privacy and the public sphere of politics, as the administrative state assumes increasing responsibility; in Jürgen Habermas, *The Structural Transformation of the Public Sphere: An Inquiry into a Category of Bourgeois Society*, trans. Thomas Burger (Boston: MIT Press, 1989).

24. Whitman, "Democratic Vistas," *Prose Works 1892*, vol. 2, ed. Floyd Stovall (New York: New York University Press, 1964), 414; Whitman, *Notes and Fragments*, ed. Richard Maurice Bucke (Ontario, Canada: A. Talbot, 1899), 169.

25. As Ed Folsom notes in *Whitman Making Books, Books Making Whitman* (Iowa City: University of Iowa Oberman Center for Advanced Study, 2005), in the 1860 *Leaves of Grass* Whitman complements the spermatic imagery of his poems with spermlike figures that sprout out of the title on the title page and reappear in titles or as erotically suggestive figures at beginnings and endings of poems and sequences throughout the volume (18).

26. Helms, "Whitman's," 185–205; Parker, "The Real," 145–60; see also Richard Tayson, "The Casualties of Walt Whitman,"

Virginia Quarterly Review 81 (Spring 2005): 79–95. For a contemporary critical attack on Whitman's "public onanism," his "public performance of what most of us would only do in private," see Robert S. Frederickson, "Public Onanism: Whitman's 'Song of Himself,'" *MLQ* 2 (June 1985): 143–60. For a discussion of the ongoing national policing of Whitman's homosexuality, see Betsy Erkkila, "Introduction: Breaking Bounds," and Jay Grossman, "Epilogue: Whitman's Centennial and the State of Whitman Studies," in *Breaking Bounds: Whitman and American Cultural Studies*, ed. Betsy Erkkila and Jay Grossman (New York: Oxford University Press, 1996), 3–20, 251–64.

27. Malcolm Cowley, *Selected Correspondence of Kenneth Burke and Malcolm Cowley: 1915–1981*, ed. Paul Jay (New York: Viking, 1988), 273.

28. For a discussion of the "resilient irreducibility" that Whitman "builds into the passionate attachments of men to men" in his poems, see Peter Coviello, "Intimate Nationality: Anonymity and Attachment in Whitman," *American Literature* 73 (March 2001): 107; see also John Vincent's examination of Whitman's oscillation "between the proffering and withholding of 'the truth' of his 'sexual identity,'" in "Rhetorical Suspense, Sexuality, and Death in Whitman's 'Calamus' Poems," *Arizona Quarterly* 56 (Spring 2000): 29–48; and Shively, who observes: "Part of the gay ambiance is to reveal yourself only to potential and desirable partners" (*Calamus Lovers*, 24).

29. Martin, *Homosexual Tradition*, 76.

30. Schmidgall describes the changes Whitman made in his poems after 1860 as "a lengthy and meticulous sexual suicide" (*Walt Whitman*, 145). See also M. Jimmie Killingsworth, who writes: "Propriety had become a central tenet for the postwar Whitman" (*Whitman's Poetry of the Body: Sexuality, Politics and the Text* [Chapel Hill: University of North Carolina Press, 1989], 148); Helms, "Whitman's," 197; and Katz: "By June 1865," he writes, "Whitman was becoming more circumspect" (*Love Stories*, 161).

31. Joseph Cady makes a similar point in "*Drum-Taps* and Nineteenth-Century Male Homosexual Literature," but he continues to distinguish between the private poet of homosexual love and the more public figure of the soldier-comrade through whom Whitman self-protectively masks his homosexual desire; in *Walt Whitman: Here and Now*, ed. Joann P. Krieg (Westport,

CT: Greenwood Press, 1985), 49–60. What I want to stress is the inseparability of the private discourses of male homosexual desire from the more public discourses of combat and democratic nationalism in Whitman's poems of the Civil War.

32. As we have come to know more about Lincoln's intimate friendship with Joshua Speed, with whom he shared a double bed in Springfield, Whitman's evocation of Lincoln as comrade and lover has come to seem particularly prescient; in fact, there may be more than we know to Whitman's "thought of him I love" and "comrade lustrous" and the sexual subculture they may have shared in wartime Washington. See, for example, Whitman's notebook entries for October 31, 1863 [Saturday] and November 1, 1863 [Sunday], in which he describes a visit to the White House: "31st Oct Called at the President's house . . . saw Mr Lincoln standing, talking with a gentleman, apparently a dear friend. Nov 1st —his face & manner have an expression & are inexpressibly sweet—one hand on his friends shoulder the other holding his hand. I love the President personally" (*Notebooks and Unpublished Prose Manuscripts*, vol. 2, ed. Edward F. Grier [New York: New York University Press, 1984], 539). Although Whitman may not have "slept over at the White House," Shively observes, "he did cruise the area by moonlight and he certainly had a crush on the Illinois Rail–Splitter" (*Calamus Lovers*, 32). Split as this note is between Whitman's passing glimpse of Lincoln with another man on Saturday and his proclamation of love for the president the following day, the note suggests that Whitman may actually have spent the night at the president's house. For Lincoln's relationship with Joshua Speed, see Charles B. Strozier, *Lincoln's Quest for Union: Public and Private Meanings* (Urbana: University of Illinois Press, 1982).

33. *Drum-Taps (1865) and Sequel to Drum-Taps (1865–1866), A Facsimile Reproduction*, ed. F. DeWolfe Miller (Gainesville, FL: Scholars' Facsimiles and Reprints, 1959), 19.

34. On June 30, 1865, Whitman was fired from his job as a clerk in the Department of the Interior when Secretary James Harlan "found" a marked copy of the 1860 *Leaves of Grass* in Whitman's desk. Although Whitman was reemployed the next day in the attorney general's office, his friend William D. O'Connor undertook an impassioned defense of the poet against charges of moral turpitude in a pamphlet entitled *The Good Gray Poet*, which was published in 1866. For a study of the erotic bonds Whitman

formed with soldiers during the Civil War, see *Drum Beats: Walt Whitman's Civil War Boy Lovers*, ed. Charley Shively (San Francisco: Gay Sunshine Press, 1989), which includes a selection of soldiers' letters written to Whitman during and after the war. See also Schmidgall, *Gay Life*, and Katz, *Love Stories*.

35. Horace Traubel, *With Walt Whitman in Camden*, vols. 1–3 (1905–1914; reprint, New York: Rowman and Littlefield, 1961), 2: 261.

36. *Walt Whitman: The Correspondence*, ed. Edwin Haviland Miller (New York: New York University Press, 1961–1977), 2: 47, 84, 104.

37. Walt Whitman, *Uncollected Poetry and Prose*, ed. Emory Holloway (Garden City, NY: Doubleday, Page, and Company, 1921), 2: 96–97.

38. Whitman, *Correspondence*, 3: 68, 215.

39. These photographs are available at the Walt Whitman Archive, http://www.whitmanarchive.org/multimedia/index.html; they are also reprinted in Ed Folsom, "Whitman's Calamus Photographs," in Erkkila and Grossman, 193–219.

40. Folsom, "Whitman's Calamus Photographs," 193–219.

41. In a series entitled "Suggestions for Posing," which was published in *Anthony's Photographic Bulletin* between 1870 and 1871, for example, seventy-one different examples of posing are suggested, but none are men together; and in a section entitled "On Groups" in the popular 1883 book *About Photography and Photographers*, Henry Baden Pritchard argues that nonfamily groups are "usually a failure as an artistic work"; cited in John Ibson, *Picturing Men: A Century of Male Relationships in Everyday American Photography* (Washington, DC: Smithsonian Institution Press, 2002), 16. As Ibson observes, the portraits of men together in front of the primarily male gaze of the studio camera in the nineteenth century reveal a world of male intimacy that "would largely disappear from view" in the late nineteenth and early twentieth centuries as taboos about male homosexuality and communality took hold in the culture.

42. "Lew is so good, so affectionate," Whitman wrote to Sawyer about visiting Lewis Brown at the Armory hospital, "when I came away, he reached up his face, I put my arm around him, and we gave each other a long kiss, half a minute long" (Whitman to Thomas Sawyer, 21 April 1863, Whitman, *Correspondence*, 1: 91).

43. Shively, *Calamus Lovers*, 54.

44. Here the distinction that Michael Warner and Lauren Berlant make between *heterosexuality* as a way of organizing sexual relations and *heteronormativity* as a way of ordering the world is useful. Whereas heterosexuality was put in place in the late nineteenth century as a way of organizing sexual relations and male and female identity, "heteronormativity" is a whole set of relations, structures, and assumptions that pervade every aspect of American life; in Lauren Berlant and Michael Warner, "Sex in Public," *Critical Inquiry* 24 (Winter 1998): 548.

45. Gay Wilson Allen argues that the "Base of All Metaphysics" moves "toward the sublimation and reinterpretation of the original personal confessions" of "Calamus," in *The New Walt Whitman Handbook* (New York: New York University Press, 1975), 133; Martin describes the poem as "a descent" from "honest statement" to "increasing vagueness" (*Homosexual Tradition*, 88); and Helms claims that, after 1860, Whitman "remained silent on the subject of homosexual love" ("Whitman's," 197). See also David Oates's reading of "The Base of All Metaphysics" in *Walt Whitman: An Encyclopedia*, ed. J. R. LeMaster and Donald D. Kummings (New York: Garland Publishing, 1998), 49–50.

46. Walt Whitman, *Notebooks*, 5: 1882. Whitman cites Plato's *Phaedrus*, in vol. 1 of Bohn's 6-volume edition of Plato, first published in 1854 (*Notebooks* 5: 1881). Martin suggests that Whitman may also have read Plato's *Symposium* in a text called "The Banquet" in *Works of Plato: A New and Literal Version*, trans. George Burges, 3: 493. Pausanias uses the term "manly" love to refer to men who "associate through the whole of life together": they are "the most manly in their disposition" and have "a manly temper and manly look" (512; cited in Martin, *Homosexual Tradition*, 226n51).

47. Although Whitman's inclusion of "the well-married husband and wife, of children and parents" in his vision of comradely love might appear to dilute or silence his emphasis on "manly love" in other "Calamus" poems, it is important to note the slipperiness of the terms husband, wife, child, and parent in his homoerotic metaphysics. Describing himself as "the new husband" to his male lovers in the "Calamus" poems, Whitman fluidly assumes the roles of mother, brother, husband, father, and bride in representing his love relationships with men in his poems.

48. Walt Whitman, *Prose Works*, 2: 466.

49. Walt Whitman, *Prose Works*, 2: 414–15; see also *Specimen*

Days (1882), in which Whitman finds among the workers and crowded city streets of "Human and Heroic New York" "a palpable outcropping of that personal comradeship I look forward to as the subtlest, strongest future hold of this many–item'd Union" (*Prose Works*, 1: 172).

50. Nancy Fraser, "Rethinking the Public Sphere: A Contribution to the Critique of Actually Existing Democracy," in *Habermas and the Public Sphere*, ed. Craig Calhoun (Boston: MIT Press, 1992), 109–42.

51. Walt Whitman, *Prose Works*, 2: 471.

52. See, for example, Gay Wilson Allen, who writes that Whitman "left convincing evidence in his notebooks that ['Enfans d'Adam'] was an after–thought, growing not from an inner compulsion but used for the strategic purpose of balancing 'Calamus'—or more accurately the cluster of twelve poems first called 'Live-Oak Leaves,' before Whitman had thought of his calamus plant symbol"; in *The Solitary Singer: A Critical Biography of Walt Whitman* (1955; New York: New York University Press, 1967), 250.

53. Whitman, *Notes and Fragments*, 169.

54. Shively, *Calamus Lovers*, 21.

55. See Robert K. Martin, "Whitman's 'Song of Myself': Homosexual Dream and Vision," *Partisan Review* 42 (1975): 80–96; and Byrne R. S. Fone, *Masculine Landscapes: Walt Whitman and the Homoerotic Text* (Carbondale: Southern Illinois University Press, 1992).

56. Walt Whitman, *Leaves of Grass*, ed. Sculley Bradley and Harold Blodgett (New York: New York University Press, 1965), 109.

57. See also Whitman's deletion of the reference to "the perfect girl" in "Enfans" 2 ("From Pent-Up Aching Rivers") and the explicit references to the female in "Enfans" 6 ("One Hour to Madness and Joy").

58. "As Adam Early in the Morning," *Leaves of Grass*, ed. Bradley and Blodgett, 111.

59. Michael Lynch, "'Here is Adhesiveness': From Friendship to Homosexuality," *Victorian Studies* (Autumn 1985): 91, 67.

60. Whitman, *Correspondence*, 3: 267 n.

61. For the single instance of erotic desire between women, see Whitman's evocation of the loving relationship between his mother and a Native American woman in "The Sleepers," *Leaves of Grass*, 424–33.

62. Unlike Symonds, who was married, closeted, and more angst–ridden about his sexual relations with working-class men, Edward Carpenter turned away from the Anglican religion, the class of his birth, and his Cambridge education to live openly with his lover, George Merrill, as a farmer in the working-class town of Sheffield in the north of England. He was a sex and labor radical, a socialist, and a feminist; he wrote books on free love, homosexuality, democracy, and spirituality, including *Days with Walt Whitman* (1906), an account of his visits with Whitman for several weeks in 1877 and 1884, and *The Intermediate Sex* (1908), a study of what he called "homogenic" or "Uranian" love between persons of the same sex.

63. Symonds was a Renaissance scholar and poet who circulated in an emergent upper-class homosocial community in late Victorian England. He wrote pioneering studies of sexual inversion, including *A Problem in Greek Ethics*, which was privately printed in 1883 and circulated in an edition of only ten copies, and *Sexual Inversion* (1897), which was co-authored with the British sexologist and social reformer Havelock Ellis. He also wrote one of the earliest biographies of Whitman, *Walt Whitman: A Study* (1893), published in London the same day that Symonds died in Rome.

64. Whitman, *Correspondence*, 5: 72–73.

65. See Havelock Ellis and John Addington Symonds, *Sexual Inversion* (London: Wilson and Macmillan, 1897). See also Martin, who emphasizes the class difference between Whitman and Symonds, and thus the ways Whitman's response to Symonds might be read as an attempt to "put on" and put down Symonds as an effete member of the British aristocracy who knows nothing about American working-class comradeship and sexuality; in "Whitman and the Politics of Identity," in *Walt Whitman: The Centennial Essays*, ed. Ed Folsom (Iowa City: University of Iowa Press, 1994), 172–81; and Doty, on the democratic difference and newness of Whitman's bonds with working-class men, 66–78.

66. Whitman, *Correspondence*, 5: 73.

67. Bucke, who first read Whitman's work in 1867, was a Canadian physician and later psychologist and spiritualist. In 1883, he published the first biography of the poet, *Walt Whitman*, much of which was written or shaped by Whitman himself. Later in *Cosmic Consciousness* (1901), Bucke represents Whitman as a higher form of moral and spiritual being, comparable to the Buddha

or Christ. The film *Beautiful Dreamers* (1992) presents a fiction-alized version of their relationship. Along with Thomas Harned and Horace Traubel, Bucke was one of Whitman's literary execu-tors, who are known as Whitman's "disciples." Born and raised in Camden, New Jersey, and befriended in his teens by Whitman, Traubel was a printer, journalist, and socialist internationalist best known for his record of conversations with Whitman, be-tween 1888 and the poet's death in 1892, in his multivolume *With Walt Whitman at Camden*.

68. Malcolm Cowley, "Walt Whitman: The Secret," *New Re-public* 114 (April 8, 1946), 481–84. For debates about Whitman's sexuality in Europe, see Sedgwick; Erkkila, *Whitman among the French*; and Grünzweig, *Constructing the German Walt Whitman*. In England between 1885 and 1894, it was still possible for the primarily middle-class group of English men known as the Eagle Street College to translate Whitman's message into a heady mix of labor radicalism, passionate attachment, and spiritual commu-nion that, in the words of Harry Cocks, substituted "inexpress-ible, spiritual communion for 'unspeakable' physical possibili-ties." "For the College," Cocks observes, "Whitman was an avatar of comradeship and the oneness of the Universe, whereas for some of their contemporaries he was simply and uncontestably a homo-sexual"; in *"Calamus* in Bolton: Spirituality and Homosexual Desire in Late Victorian England," *Gender and History* 13 (Au-gust 2001): 192, 217–18; see also Michael Robertson, *Worshipping Walt: The Whitman Disciples* (Princeton, NJ: Princeton Univer-sity Press, 2008).

69. See Richard Maurice Bucke, *Cosmic Consciousness: A Study of the Evolution of the Human Mind* (1901, New York: Dutton, 1969); Bucke, ed., *Calamus: A Series of Letters Written During the Years 1868–1880 by Walt Whitman to a Young Friend (Peter Doyle)* (Boston: Laurens Maynard, 1897); F. O. Matthiessen, *American Renaissance: Art and Expression in the Age of Emerson and Whit-man* (New York: Oxford University Press, 1941); James E. Miller Jr., "Whitman's 'Calamus': The Leaf and the Root," *PMLA* 72 (March 1957): 249–71; and Edwin Haviland Miller, *Walt Whit-man's Poetry: A Psychological Journey* (Boston: Houghton Mifflin, 1968).

70. Gavin Arthur, *The Circle of Sex* (New Hyde Park, NY: Uni-versity Books, 1966), 135.

71. Gavin Arthur, *Gay Sunshine* 35 (Winter 1978): 29.

72. In a *Gay Sunshine* interview with Allen Young, Allen Ginsberg says that he slept with Neal Cassady, "who slept with Gavin Arthur, who slept with Edward Carpenter, who slept with Whitman." Ginsberg evokes this as part of a Whitmanian or gay generation, sexual, poetic, democratic, and spiritual: "So this is in a sense the line of transmission," he says; "that's an interesting thing to have as part of the mythology"; in *Gay Sunshine Interviews*, vol. 1, ed. Winston Leyland (San Francisco: Gay Sunshine Press, 1978), 106.

"Calamus" and Whitman's Man Love
A Selected Bibliography

Berlant, Lauren, and Michael Warner. "Sex in Public."
  Critical Inquiry 24 (Winter 1998): 547–66.
Berman, Richard, and David Groff, eds. *Walt Whitman's Men:
  Walt Whitman's Calamus Poems Celebrated by Contemporary
  Photographers*. New York: Universe Publishing, 1996.
Bowers, Fredson, ed. *Whitman's Manuscripts: Leaves of Grass
  (1860), A Parallel Text*. Chicago: University of Chicago Press,
  1955.
———. "Whitman's Manuscripts of the Original 'Calamus'
  Poems." *Studies in Bibliography* 6 (1953): 257–65.
Cady, Joseph. "*Drum-Taps* and Nineteenth-Century Male
  Homosexual Literature." In *Walt Whitman: Here and Now*,
  ed. Joann P. Krieg. Westport, CT: Greenwood Press, 1985.
  49–60.
———. "Not Happy in the Capital: Homosexuality and the
  'Calamus' Poems." *American Studies* 19 (Fall 1978): 5–22.
Carpenter, Edward. *Days with Walt Whitman*. London: G. Allen,
  1906.
Champagne, John. "Walt Whitman, Our Great Gay Poet?"
  Journal of Homosexuality 55 (2008): 648–64.
Cocks, Harry. "*Calamus* in Bolton: Spirituality and Homosexual
  Desire in Late Victorian England." *Gender and History* 13
  (August 2001): 191–223.
Coviello, Peter. "Intimate Nationality: Anonymity and
  Attachment in Whitman." *American Literature* 73 (March
  2001): 85–119.
Cowley, Malcolm. "Walt Whitman: The Secret." *New Republic*
  114 (8 April 1946): 481–84.
Doty, Mark. "Form, Eros, and the Unspeakable: Whitman's
  Stanzas." *Virginia Quarterly Review* 81 (Spring 2005): 66–78.
Erkkila, Betsy. "Public Love: Whitman and Political Theory."
  In *Whitman East and West: New Contexts for Reading Walt
  Whitman*, ed. Ed Folsom. Iowa City: University of Iowa
  Press, 2002. 115–44.

————. "Whitman and the Homosexual Republic." In *Walt Whitman: The Centennial Essays*, ed. Ed Folsom. Iowa City: University of Iowa Press, 1994. 153–71.

————. *Whitman the Political Poet*. New York: Oxford University Press, 1989.

————, and Jay Grossman, eds. *Breaking Bounds: Whitman and American Cultural Studies*. New York: Oxford University Press, 1996.

Folsom, Ed. "Whitman's Calamus Photographs." In *Breaking Bounds: Walt Whitman and American Cultural Studies*, ed. Betsy Erkkila and Jay Grossman. New York: Oxford University Press, 1996. 193–219.

————, and Kenneth M. Price. *Re-Scripting Walt Whitman: An Introduction to His Life and Work*. Malden, MA: Blackwell, 2005.

Fone, Byrne R. S. *Masculine Landscapes: Walt Whitman and the Homoerotic Text*. Carbondale: Southern Illinois University Press, 1992.

Giantvalley, Scott. "Recent Whitman Studies and Homosexuality." *Cabirion and Gay Books Bulletin* 12 (Spring/Summer 1985): 14–16.

Grossman, Jay. "'The Evangel-Poem of Comrades and of Love': Revising Whitman's Republicanism." *American Transcendental Quarterly* 4 (September 1990): 201–18.

Halperin, David H. *One Hundred Years of Homosexuality*. New York: Routledge, 1990.

Helms, Alan. "'Hints . . . Faint Clues and Indirections': Whitman's Homosexual Disguises." In *Walt Whitman: Here and Now*, ed. Joann P. Krieg. Westport, CT: Greenwood, 1985. 61–67.

————. "Whitman's 'Live Oak with Moss.'" In *The Continuing Presence of Walt Whitman: The Life after the Life*, ed. Robert K. Martin. Iowa City: University of Iowa Press, 1992. 185–205.

Hyde, Lewis. *The Gift: Imagination and the Erotic Life of Property*. New York: Vantage, 1983.

Katz, Jonathan Ned. *Gay American History: Lesbians and Gay Men in the U.S.A.* New York: Thomas Y. Crowell, 1976.

————. *Love Stories: Sex between Men before Homosexuality*. Chicago: University of Chicago Press, 2001.

Keller, Karl. "Walt Whitman and the Queening of America."
   American Poetry 1 (Fall 1983): 4–26.
Killingsworth, M. Jimmie. "Sentimentality and Homosexuality
   in Whitman's 'Calamus.'" *ESQ* 29 (1983): 144–53.
———. "Whitman and the Gay American Ethos." In
   A Historical Guide to Walt Whitman, ed. David S. Reynolds.
   New York: Oxford University Press, 2000. 121–51.
Lynch, Michael. "'Here Is Adhesiveness': From Friendship to
   Homosexuality." *Victorian Studies* (Autumn 1985): 67–96.
Martin, Robert K. "Conversion and Identity: The 'Calamus'
   Poems." *Walt Whitman Review* 25 (June 1979): 59–66.
———. "The Disseminal Whitman: A Deconstructive Approach
   to '*Enfans d'Adam*' and '*Calamus*.'" In *Approaches to Teaching
   Whitman's "Leaves of Grass"*, ed. Donald Kummings. New
   York: Modern Language Association, 1990. 74–80.
———. *The Homosexual Tradition in American Poetry*. Austin:
   University of Texas Press, 1979.
———. "Melting in Fondness: Love in Whitman's Poems of the
   1870's." *Calamus* 21 (December 1981): 13–23.
———. "Whitman and the Politics of Identity." *Walt Whitman:
   The Centennial Essays*, ed. Ed Folsom. Iowa City: University
   of Iowa Press, 1994. 172–81.
———. "Whitman's 'Song of Myself': Homosexual Dream and
   Vision." *Partisan Review* 42 (1975): 80–96.
Maslan, Mark. *Whitman Possessed: Poetry, Sexuality, and Popular
   Authority*. Baltimore: Johns Hopkins University Press, 2001.
Miller, James E., Jr. "Whitman's 'Calamus': The Leaf and the
   Root." *PMLA* 72 (March 1957): 249–71.
Moon, Michael. *Disseminating Whitman: Revision and
   Corporeality in "Leaves of Grass."* Cambridge, MA: Harvard
   University Press, 1991.
———. "Rereading Whitman under Pressure of AIDS: His Sex
   Radicalism and Ours." In *The Continuing Presence of Walt
   Whitman: The Life after the Life*, ed. Robert K. Martin. Iowa
   City: University of Iowa Press, 1992. 53–66.
Newfield, Christopher. "Democracy and Male Homoeroticism."
   Yale Journal of Criticism 6 (Fall 1993): 29–62.
Olsen-Smith, Steven. "'Live Oak, with Moss,' 'Calamus,' and
   'Children of Adam.'" In *A Companion to Walt Whitman*,
   ed. Donald D. Kummings. Malden, MA: Blackwell, 2006.
   508–21.

———, and Hershel Parker. "'Live Oak, with Moss' and 'Calamus': Textual Inhibitions in Whitman Criticism." *Walt Whitman Quarterly Review* 14 (Spring 1997): 153–65.

Parker, Hershel. "The Real 'Live Oak, with Moss': Straight Talk about Whitman's 'Gay Manifesto.'" *Nineteenth-Century Literature* 51 (September 1996): 145–60.

Pollak, Vivian. *The Erotic Whitman*. Berkeley: University of California Press, 2000.

Robertson, Michael. *Worshipping Walt: The Whitman Disciples*. Princeton, NJ: Princeton University Press, 2008.

Schmidgall, Gary. *Walt Whitman: A Gay Life*. New York: Dutton, 1997.

Scholnick, Robert J. "The Texts and Contexts of 'Calamus': Did Whitman Censor Himself in 1860?" *Walt Whitman Quarterly Review* 21 (Winter 2004): 109–30.

———. "'This Terrible, Irrepressible Yearning': Whitman's Poetics of Love." In *American Declarations of Love*, ed. Anna Massa. New York: St. Martin's Press, 1990. 46–67.

Sedgwick, Eve Kosofsky. "Toward the Twentieth Century: English Readers of Whitman." In *Between Men: English Literature and Male Homosocial Desire*. New York: Columbia University Press, 1985. 201–17.

Shively, Charley, ed. *Calamus Lovers: Walt Whitman's Working-Class Camerados*. San Francisco: Gay Sunshine Press, 1987.

———, ed. *Drum Beats: Walt Whitman's Civil War Boy Lovers*. San Francisco: Gay Sunshine Press, 1989.

Stansell, Christine. "Whitman at Pfaffs: Commercial Culture, Literary Life, and New York Bohemia at Mid-Century." *Walt Whitman Quarterly Review* 10 (Winter 1993): 107–26.

Symonds, John Addington. *Walt Whitman: A Study*. London: John C. Nimmo, 1893.

Tayson, Richard. "The Casualties of Walt Whitman." *Virginia Quarterly Review* 81 (Spring 2005): 79–95.

Vincent, John. "Rhetorical Suspense, Sexuality, and Death in Whitman's 'Calamus' Poems." *Arizona Quarterly* 56 (Spring 2000): 29–48.

Warner, Michael. "Whitman Drunk." In *Breaking Bounds: Whitman and American Cultural Studies*, ed. Betsy Erkkila and Jay Grossman. New York: Oxford University Press, 1996. 30–43.

Whitman, Walt. *Calamus: A Series of Letters Written during the Years 1868–1880 by Walt Whitman to a Young Friend (Peter Doyle)*, ed. Richard Maurice Bucke. Boston: Small, Maynard, 1897.

Winwar, Frances. "Whitman's 'Calamus' Poems." *Princeton University Library Chronicle* 3 (February 1942): 66–68.

The Iowa Whitman Series

Conserving Walt Whitman's Fame:
Selections from Horace Traubel's "Conservator," 1890–1919,
edited by Gary Schmidgall

Democratic Vistas: The Original Edition in Facsimile,
by Walt Whitman, edited by Ed Folsom

Intimate with Walt:
Selections from Whitman's Conversations with Horace Traubel,
1888–1892, edited by Gary Schmidgall

Leaves of Grass, 1860:
The 150th Facsimile Anniversary Edition, by Walt Whitman,
edited by Jason Stacy

The Pragmatic Whitman: Reimagining American Democracy,
by Stephen John Mack

Supplement to "Walt Whitman: A Descriptive Bibliography,"
edited by Joel Myerson

Transatlantic Connections: Whitman U.S., Whitman U.K.,
by M. Wynn Thomas

Visiting Walt: Poems Inspired by the
Life and Work of Walt Whitman,
edited by Sheila Coghill and Thom Tammaro

Walt Whitman: The Correspondence, Volume VII,
edited by Ted Genoways

Walt Whitman and the Class Struggle, by Andrew Lawson

Walt Whitman and the Earth: A Study in Ecopoetics,
by M. Jimmie Killingsworth

Walt Whitman, Where the Future Becomes Present,
edited by David Haven Blake and Michael Robertson

*Walt Whitman's Songs of Male Intimacy and Love:
"Live Oak, with Moss" and "Calamus,"*
edited by Betsy Erkkila

*Whitman East and West:
New Contexts for Reading Walt Whitman,*
edited by Ed Folsom